BRAIN-TALK MEETS GOD-TALK

BRAIN-TALK MEETS GOD-TALK

How neurology and theology merge to rewire your brain and restore your peace.

STEVE BAKER

Printed in the United States of America
Published by Author Academy Elite
P.O. Box 43, Powell, OH 43035
www.AuthorAcademyElite.com

Library of Congress Cataloging 2019931734

Softcover: 978-1-64085-572-4
Hardcover: 978-1-64085-573-1
E-book: 978-1-64085-574-8
Audiobook:
Available in hardcover, softcover, e-book, and audiobook

To the redeemed of the Lord—for the healing of their wounded souls.

Mental pain is less dramatic than physical pain, but it is more common and also more hard to bear. The frequent attempt to conceal mental pain increases the burden: it is easier to say "My tooth is aching" than to say "My heart is broken."

C.S. Lewis, *The Problem of Pain*

CONTENTS

Part 1: Sparks and Storms

Part 2: Rewire and Recover

LIST OF ILLUSTRATIONS AND THE ARTISTS

Book cover design by Ronald Cruz, Cruzialdesigns at 99designs.com

"Search for Anthony"; Pottin and Bida; *St Catherines Monastery*, Mount Sinai, Egypt, 1864. Shutterstock.com

"Breathing Exercise" by Austeja. Fiverr.com

"Brain-talk: Serenity vs. Anxiety"; *Cross section of human brain* by Blamb. Shutterstock.com

"Shield of the Trinity" (English) from "Scutum Fidei"

"Be still" by Austeja. Fiverr.com

"Book with Binder Clips" by Austeja. Fiverr.com

"Book on the Table" by Austeja. Fiverr.com

ACKNOWLEDGMENTS: COMPASSIONATE SOULS

Kathy Baker, my wife of nearly 40 years. She never experienced depression, but through her love and prayers, aided me in all hope, confidence, and courage.

Mark Stevenson, my friend. Not only is he an example of a soul rescued from depression, but he also shared his courage with me for hours as we aggressively attacked Iowa's bicycling trails.

Jim Epp, my friend. He exercised his gift of compassion by calling me every day with encouragement and hope throughout my darkest days.

Dr. Joe Barrash, the neuropsychologist from the University of Iowa Hospital and Clinics. His kind words unlocked great possibilities for my body, mind, and soul.

Dr. Ron Pick, my physician for 30 years. He knows the value of nurturing a healthy body, sound mind, and content soul.

Rev. Mike Rose, my pastor. He shepherded me to safety, for he knows what traumatized souls in churches need.

Rev. Thomas Clegg, pastor-prophet and cyclist. He's the one who said, "Depression is your gift."

Gabor George Burt, mastermind of innovation. In our conversation, he identified how I merged neurology and theology, and then said, "Write your book."

ABOUT THIS BOOK

It's About Mental Storms and Recovery

Brain-talk Meets God-talk has two parts. The first part is a story narrative. Some of it is fictional, taking you back in time to an early century of Christianity and then with a time leap forward, the main character reclaims the forgotten gift of the Fourth Century.

I include glimpses of my depression to tell a few storm stories because you might relate to them. Telling a story is more fun to write and, perhaps, easier to digest than the technical writing found in most instruction manuals.

The second part is an instruction manual. As a technical writer, I endeavor to write with clarity to tell you what to do. I give step-by-step instructions with illustrations.

You can jump into Part 2 without reading the stories, for you can take time to read those later. The Part 1 stories are, however, designed to walk you into Part 2.

It's About You and God

Brain-talk Meets God-talk is a different type of book. It's about you and your need for hope, and most importantly, it is about God who gives you that hope to restore your peace.

It's about your connection with God for a brief 20 minutes a day to bring healing to your body (brain), mind (thinking), and soul (life). This book delivers Daily Focus meditations structured to make the most of your time to address the entirety of you as a human being—an image of God.

This is not a memoir about my depression. Almost all memoirs and books that wrangle with the sensitive topic of depression begin with the capital I—"I think," "I thought," "I feel," "I felt,"—and then you observe how the author handled the problem of depression.

This book is not a journal with "here's my problem (sad me) and how I found relief."

It took three years to write this book. I started it when depression was stealing vitality from my life. But as I applied the meditation techniques I developed, my life changed from perpetual frowning and blank stares to spontaneous smiles and reconnecting to life. Because I applied familiar theology (God-talk) and merged it with what I understood of neurology (Brain-talk) the result is now a surprisingly helpful meditation practice. I continue to practice what I composed, and now I want to share it with you.

It's About Depression and Meditation

It seems that everyone wants to tell you to meditate, but you hesitate. You think it may be wrong, and you rightfully discern that some meditation practices are wrong. Yoga and Zen come to mind, and you are uncomfortable with those things.

Friends will present you with Bible verses to memorize and ponder, but your mind wanders. People tell you to pray more, read the Bible more, but you see no progress in your efforts to pull out of clinical depression. If these methods truly worked, you should be better by now, but you're not.

Leave behind the traps of Yoga, Buddha, Zen, or anything else that is not Christian. Move forward to meditation that is uniquely Christian, but it is not done in the way others have told you. This book shows you exactly how to meditate without the slightest hint of something from eastern religions.

This book exalts our Triune God—Father, Son, and Holy Spirit. As you acknowledge God's presence and declare God's truth about himself, and purposefully apply neurological methods, your brain will change. It's called neuroplasticity. Your brain will be re-wired with good thoughts about our good God.

The God of real peace and the creator of your soul is the true focus in this method. Scripture verses are the foundational truths presented in this book, but these verses are not thrown at you to make you feel guilty or shameful for thinking dark thoughts. You are not required to memorize the verses.

It's About Our Christian Faith

Nothing in this book will violate your love for Jesus. There are no strange sitting positions, no whacky words, and no heretical teaching of becoming one with the universe. It is explicitly written for believers in Christ who are indwelt by the Holy Spirit.

This book does not borrow from any non-Christian religious practices. Christians of any denomination and in any part of the world will find nothing here to doubt our Triune God (Father, Son, and Holy Spirit) or speak falsely about the character of God as revealed in the Bible. No controversial doctrines are brought up. God will speak to you through the Scriptures and the snippets of truth.

It's About Our Roots

True Biblical meditation has roots in Judaism. Thousands of years ago, our Jewish relatives knew how to meditate from the Book of the Law day and night. In the early centuries after Christ, Christians may have adopted similar methods, but almost 2,000 years later, we've forgotten how they may have meditated. Over the centuries, we have neglected our roots.

Christians have let other religions claim that meditation is something they owned first. Meditation did not originate with them. It is a practice found in the Old Testament long before India's Hinduism and Asia's Buddhism.

This book is written for Christians who suffer from depression, yet it is for any Christ-redeemed soul who has been advised to meditate. Sadly, what passes for Christian meditation today are devotional writings that do not offer the means of re-wiring the brain with new neural pathways. Real meditation puts you in a calm state—serenity—to let God work at restoring your soul.

Now is the right time to begin those changes.

It's About Time

It's about time you spend with God—20 minutes a day for 36 days; long enough for you to perceive changes in your brain, your thoughts, and your life.

It's about the time necessary to reclaim serenity, or if that's been elusive for most your life, to finally find it.

It's about a brief exchange of time for lifetime benefits. Besides stress management, you may even experience healthy weight loss because there is a lesser amount of cortisol coursing through your system.

It's about time to be lifted out of darkness.

"Let the words of my mouth and the meditation of my heart be acceptable in your sight, O LORD, my rock and my redeemer" (Psalm 19:14).

PART 1

SPARKS AND STORMS

ANCIENT SANDSTORMS

Weather Report

Khamsin: From the Arabic word for "fifty", these sand-filled windstorms blow sporadically in Egypt over a fifty-day period in spring. The storm can last for several hours as it carries desert sand and dust with wind speeds up to 87 miles per hour (140 kph) and the humidity in that area drops below 5%.

Simoom: From the Arabic verb "to poison," these dust-laden desert cyclones blast with temperatures that may exceed 129 °F (54 °C) The name means "poison wind" because, at its sudden onset, it can cause heat stroke. The hot wind with its clouds of dust and sand can suffocate humans and animals.

Presume the Desert

Desert dry is nose bleed dry. The old man's nostrils hurt to breathe in the excessive heat without filtering it through the scarf dangling from his head wrap. He wheezes in rhythm to his feet shuffling in the dust.

It is the Coptic month of Parmouti, but its natural heat during the Roman calendar months of April to May had stayed away. It seemed more like pleasant February and March in AD 356.

When the spring winds of northern Egypt didn't blow, Anthony, at 105 years old, regarded the subtle climate change as his sign to venture back to his hideaway in the Eastern Desert.

The hot winds returned during his last week of solitude.

Hermit's Head Talk

Fool of a monk. Presumed on the desert. Know better. Twice the age of the bishops in Alexandria. Know the desert's ways.

Shuffle and breath. Shuffle and breath. He doesn't waste the energy to talk out loud. The cadence of his steady gait triggers his memory of an Egypt in bondage to Rome's pagan rule.

It hurt. Egypt under Roman pagans. Hurt like this desert today. Offensive and mean.

Shuffle, breath; shuffle, breath.

Know the troubles. Saw the hurts. Told the bishops. Too young or don't remember.

He turns his gaze toward the north, half expecting the glint of helmets, spears, and swinging swords from behind shields!

Maybe not now, and not Rome. Pendulums of politics and culture can swing away from respect. Always brutal.

Desert Escape

Anthony's past few weeks of escape into the desert urges him to pray, contemplate, and meditate. He loves the solitude and he hears from God without distractions. It seems that God pulls—almost drags—him out to this desolate place.

Obedience begets clarity; disobedience—not so much. Nothing left to go back to.

He had given everything away to a poor family, including his newly made mats weaved by his own hands.

Last Day

This is Anthony's last day and night away from the oasis. But just in case he misunderstood God, he had arranged for the Arab camel driver to come back in the morning after the next full moon shone in the sky.

His wobbly legs tip his body a bit.

Full moon tonight. Always wobbly with the moon.

The late afternoon sun cast shadows to the side of the stony path. Heat distortion creates a rippling effect above the dust, and as he looks back, he squints as his gaze focuses on his fresh tracks that lead away from the wasteland. Facing forward, he recognizes his foot prints from earlier in the afternoon.

Halfway—maybe.

He further slows his pace to maneuver through sharp rocks. The small stones press like little coals into his sandals.

He holds a small metal shovel in his left hand and points it away from his clothes. He had buried his personal dirt, now baking under the surface of sand and rocks, trapping the scent that would attract animals.

Respect the desert. Respect life. Respect self.

He takes his clean right-hand fingers, thin and leathery, and pulls his turban forward to shade his eyes.

It seemed like overnight the desert became a potter's kiln. Though he experienced sunbaking for a century, this furnace-like air scorches up his legs and zaps his strength.

He sees shade by the steep bluff. The ridge shows a rock wall with an exposed concave depression, and within it, a small ledge invites Anthony to get out of the sunlight and sit in its shadow. But to get there, he walks around and over big rocks. It demands that he keep his balance as he extends a sure foot to maneuver the slope.

Loose stones fool his eyes and feet, but the view of the wall's darker area pulls at him. In the shade, he thanks God for providing the small comfort for his frail body.

He sets down the shovel near his feet then backs up to feel the rock's blunt edge bump against his backside below his hips.

Perfect. Just enough headroom. Enough space to slide back.

He loosens the strings of his wide leather belt wrapped around his midsection. Though it braces him to an erect posture for prayer and meditation, it restricts his movements. He scoots back to get his legs up and over the edge.

Miscalculated

He thirsts for sips of water reserved in a goatskin bottle back in the coolest part of the cave. He clamps his hands to his forehead.

Miscalculated. Of course, the heat would return. Heat, water supply, and thirst. What could go wrong? Sure, know better.

His cup hit the bottom of the large clay pot days ago.

A sandstorm had kept him inside the cave for a few days. He usually manages the effects of strong winds, but his bony frame trembles as he walks through the hazy air and around the newly dusted rocks. Those settled fines make the stones slippery.

Can't afford to fall. Shout, "I've fallen ... can't get up!" to no one.

He sits on the rock ledge pouting his lips.

Not so tough anymore. All afternoon for this wasteland hike.

His body coaxes him to shift weight off his bottom, so he slumps over just enough. He pulls off his turban and rolls it up to be his neck pillow.

Rest is a good plan.

He is backside down on solid rock and drifts off to sleep.

He wakes long after sunset. It is dark. The remote desert night displays a cloudless sky as a pristine moon glow shines over the nightscape. It is bright enough for him to perceive the gap for his path back to his cave, but his night vision fails him. A shadow from a rock or a hole in the ground looks the same.

Might as well go blindfolded. Start now. Sunrise at the cave. Confidence. Walk blind. Can be done. Must be going.

He pulls at the lacing of his belt to start the trek.

Meet the camel driver at daylight. Have hope, be confident. Be strong and take courage. Now move.

He wiggles to angle his legs over the rock ledge. He slides his legs to the ground with gravity's assistance. The pressure of his feet touching the ground urges him to walk.

He takes his second step and hears the small shovel clink and crunch the gravel.

His ankle twists. Snaps.

Keep Breathing

The fall, lasting one second, seems in Anthony's mind like a slow downward float in the darkness. The adrenaline release dims his brain's frontal lobe, so within the time dilatation, he reviews exactly what happened. He slams to the ground.

Fool! Foolish old man! Clumsy! Clumsy old fool!

Pain scrambles his reasoning. He turns over on his back and sees the moon and stars, but his judgment of time and place isn't as prominent as the rush of pain up his leg.

Can't see the damage.

He violates his self-imposed vow of silence with the movement of his leg.

"AYAAH! BROKEN!"

Searing pain spikes up from the ankle to the hip each time Anthony lifts his body to crawl back onto the ledge. He gets there, but every part of his garment looks like he dusted it for camouflage in the night. He settles once more within the rock wall's depression.

He bundles up his turban again, this time to support his swollen ankle. His thirst intensifies.

Can't spit. Can't see straight.

Fractured leg. Nausea. A few more bruises erupt as the adrenaline wears off. Again, he speaks out loud, but the words bite into his conscience; words he often shares with disciples as they go through trials.

"Expect temptation to your last breath."

Plans Change

He loosens the lacing of his thick belt and removes it. From his tunic falls a familiar string of green jasper stones connected to a small wooden cross. It drops beside him.

He never purposefully carries the string of beads into the wasteland, yet here it is at his side. It was nestled into the fold of his garment and stayed there—up to that moment.

Of all times. Of all places.

He grasps the beads by the small wooden cross, kisses it almost as if he might suck water from the string of small stones. Then came ... clarity.

These beads—the final battle. God's Providence. It controls the universe. Present everywhere.

His own words now test him with either a preamble for a victory or a silly saying for the enemy to mock. Anthony furrows his brow and tilts his head as if to respond to a voice. But no one talks, no one debates, no one counters his soft eloquence as a desert sage.

Tell a story, make a point; make a point, tell a story.

Guilt, Shame, Darkness

The pain intensifies: the leg, his head, and throat.

The stalking demons know. They will test. They come when most weak.

The blackness around him thickens as an unseen force of darkness—an evil presence—encapsulates his little niche. An odor of decay rises up his nostrils. The moonlight dims like an oil lamp burning its last drops.

This is the last test to the last breath.

His throat tightens. He tries to swallow, but his larynx is like a stone in his throat. He presses fingers to his Adam's apple to move it slightly.

Can't talk. Can't pray ... praise.

Visible inside his mind are faces, one after another; faces with frowns: his sister as he sends her to a convent; his tutors scowling as he sits in front of a blank slate. Then mocking faces: young friends, adults in beautiful attire. He then hears the forgotten laughter intended to embarrass him.

It's time to fight. Oh, God!

The invisible fingers release the catch in his throat, and he coughs to clear his voice.

He starts a monologue, similar to one he shared with friends and lifts his head as he speaks toward the dark presence.

"The person who abides in solitude and quiet is delivered from fighting three battles: hearing, speech, and sight. Then there remains one battle to fight—the battle of the heart."

He stares into the darkness.

No answer. Caught it off guard. Took it off its plan. Now, stronger.

"Even so, I choose two of those assaults tonight for the battle of the heart. I charge with the bold blade of my tongue to receive in my ears my speech that declares God's truth. This emblazons my heart. This is the way to restore a wounded soul."

As Anthony touches two fingers and a thumb to his forehead to cross himself, a straining voice squeals out from a blacker hole of darkness in front of him.

"It ... beginss."

Death's Voice

"I challenge you, devil. I will speak first."

He scoots back a bit more, adjusting his posture to help him breathe deep. His leg protests. His gritty fingers scrape across the small Coptic cross that dangles from the string of beads. From his dry throat, he releases quiet praise.

"Because of the Cross, glory to God forever."

The Father is satisfied with the Son's payment for sins. Because of the Cross, the Holy Spirit is forever present—within.

He doesn't pause between the cross and a bead. He moves his fingers and inhales deeply, slowly. As he speaks, his exhale is as steady and slow as the inhale. His voice is no stronger than a mutter.

"In the presence of the Father, and of the Son, and of the Holy Spirit, one God."

Safe ... strong ... secure. It can't reach the heart through the Trinity.

In the distance, an animal barks and hisses.

Rüppel's fox? The sly and tricky sand fox. It hosts a demon assigned to torment. Poor beast. It will ... attack!

He raises his arms to his face, a quick reflex to ward off the sharp teeth.

It aims for the face. Then the throat. Keep arms tight and no more scars.

Nothing. Then a voice squeaks close by. It's a staccato-style speech threatening with half-barks and little cries. It resembles an Egyptian dialect.

It whines, "I ... won't ... bite ... you. You ... will ...die."

Anthony lowers his arms and tilts his head. His old ears strain to hear the voice again.

Under his tunic, he touches the scars from previous animal attacks. Inside his skull, he acknowledges the mind-scars of hurts, failures, and disappointments.

The demon weaponized this animal to talk—to the mind. Stretches its vocal cords; flaps its tongue over canine teeth. The tongue drips with death!

The voice whines again. "God ... iss ... not ... good. God ... not ... lovess ... you."

"So what?"

Anthony clutches his set of beads firmly, not with the caress merchants use to judge fine pearls, but with the grip of a fisherman who grabs a full and twisted net. He finds the largest bead and squeezes it tight, pressing it into the center of his palm with his middle finger. A nerve fires up his arm, and he breathes deep.

Tighter. Harder. Remember truth. Think truth.

His full fist compresses the whole cluster, scraping beads against beads. They make a scratching and grating sound. He releases the pressure and pulls a breath to speak to the darkness.

"God knows all things; God is present everywhere; God is all powerful. This is my premise for battle."

An immediate attack. Invisible fiery darts composed of words pulse with a melodic whine into Anthony's ears.

"God … forget … you. God … not … ssee … you. God … not … find … you."

The words 'forget … not see … not find' conjure up memories in images: lonely wanderings around his parents' house after their deaths; running into the desert night feeling guilty for their deaths; getting lost in the desert.

But Anthony remembers a Hebrew text read to him by a rabbi. The same text came to him from the Septuagint, the Greek translation from Hebrew. A mysterious merchant in Alexandria read it to him. The same text came to mind, this time from a Coptic priest who read it in a dialect similar to his own.

Light returned to his mind. In his darkest moment, when shame followed his guilt, in his heart language he delivers the Word of God exactly as it was read to him:

"Yahweh's eyes scan the whole world to find those whose hearts are committed to him."

God remembers ME. God sees ME. God finds ME. The fight is on!

"Sso what?" mocks the dark fox.

"God sees the whole world, but God finds me."

Anthony moves his thumb to pinch the next bead. He slides his fingers over and breathes deeply.

The touchable stimulation at his fingertips keeps his focus on the truth from Scripture. He speaks again but adds a theological underscore, the first person of the Trinity.

"The Father sees the world."

He holds the next bead and slowly inhales. He quietly voices the truth but augments it with his personal statement.

Each bead tells a story. Each bead makes a statement.

"Father sees me."

He moves fingers to the next bead and breathes. "Father sees me." His fingers squeeze each bead as they slide down the whole line. He returns, bead by bead, with the same phrase until his fingers touch the cross.

He hesitates. Stops. Before he executes a second tour of the beads with the second person of the Trinity, the demon interrupts.

The musky odor of the fox enters his nostrils and moist air puffs on the back of his neck.

Inflamed Heart

The evil voice hisses into Anthony's ear, "God … ssee you … worthless … ssoul."

Don't argue.

"You … sstupid. God … think you … sstupid. Can't … read … can't write."

The words 'stupid … can't read … can't write' trigger the feelings of humiliation. An image of a scroll forms in his mind and all the words swim off the papyrus. Faces of scribes and priests appear—and mock him when they hand him a stylus and request that he write out his questions.

Make this foul thing stop … and listen … to Scripture's truth.

Anthony moves his fingers again to resume a tour up and down the beads. Slowly. Thoughtfully. Methodically.

There will be no pause between stanzas.

"Your beads … funny. You break … beadss. I laughss."

The demon stepped in it. Here is truth.

"The Father strengthened committed hearts … Father strengthens my heart."

He tours the beads completely.

Don't stop.

"The Son strengthened committed hearts … Jesus strengthens my heart."

Another tour without stopping.

Third stanza, Lord. Inflame the heart.

Solitary, but not alone in the most desolate region on earth, he speaks of the Spirit, by the Spirit, and in the Spirit, and the All-powerful God joins Anthony's voice. The whispers make a duet like recited poetry.

"The Holy Spirit strengthened committed hearts."

Slice the devil's lies, Sword of the Spirit.

Then Anthony wields the words as the Spirit's sword, freshly forged, still vibrating and red-hot off the anvil. Again, it's only a whisper, but each touch of a bead signals a deep breath and a statement of truth.

"Holy Spirit strengthens my heart."

Thirty beads. Done.

He lies still, and his mind rests. Just as each of the devil's statements of un-truth pulled memories of the past, some buried in the crevices of Anthony's brain for years, truth's reward is simple: lies slashed to pieces.

His bruised finger pokes the tip of the cross. No more beads; no more breaths, but there is peace. Mind, body, and soul at rest. His brain senses no stress.

Passed the test. Need rest. Rest.

The moon's glow returns and sweet night air surrounds Anthony. Gravel rattles down from a distant slope as the fox scampers away from the human.

Anthony gently traces his fingers over his swollen leg but stops as he feels the sharp bump of the fractured bone so close to the skin. He touches his throat and forces a moan; not for the pain but victory.

He lay motionless on the rock slab. From the ledge in the cove, he no longer sees the moon, but he sees everything by its light.

He rewards himself with sleep.

Consumed by the Desert

He snorts and wakes. An arid and oppressive heat with dust tickles up his nostrils. It is daylight but impossible to know what hour. The wind gusts increase and the sky turns tan and pale brown. He closes his eyes tight.

The crevice shelters him to some extent, but it doesn't muffle the roar entering his consciousness.

No common sandstorm. Resting in the path of simoom— "poison wind"!

The desert cyclone hisses a killer's threat into his ears, "I will trade your water for dust. Your nose and mouth are mine, so breathe and eat this!"

Yield.

He twitches only a cheek muscle from behind his dust-caked beard as he knows God's glorious purpose for the *simoom*. The wind whistles to say, "Come up here!"

The whirling gusts intensify. The impersonal blast fails to rip the beads from his hand, and the wind seems to coax his voice out from the back of his throat as grit pecks his face.

He whispers without moving his stiffened lips. The words are audible only to the Omniscient God who transcends storms, deserts, earth, and time.

"Sovereign ... Lord ... take ... my ... soul ... restored ... with ... wind ... send ... song ... future ... gift...."

Loosened rubble and sand fell to encase the body as the *simoom* changes the landscape.

ANOTHER KHAMSIN

The Angel's Task

Anthony choked his last breath as a prayer. That breath depleted the remainder of Anthony's physical strength.

The angel assigned to Anthony touched its light to the old man's wrinkled hands clumped with age spots. It felt the last beat of the bodily heart. Then it shrouded the old man's frail body with light as desert dust and flying debris collected in the small cove.

The body didn't body jerk or spasm; it was worn out, sick, then lifeless. At that moment, Anthony was fully aware that his earthly time had just finished as his immaterial being rested with full consciousness. He was at peace.

Time stopped for Anthony since his body no longer had any significance. Also, he no longer needed his eyes to see, nor did he need a physical brain to interpret the electrical impulses that gave him vision. He could see and hear, but he could not move. He then sensed light.

The light came from the angel. It had manipulated its body to a dome of light that covered Anthony's body. The dome became a weave of light that resembled fine floss like a spider's web. When it molded into a spherical shape and shrank, it enmeshed the chest and head of the dead body. It then penetrated through the flesh and bones until it flashed brightly as it connected to the human's soul.

The lattice of light clutched and lifted Anthony's soul with the same tender care a young girl shows when she steals a kitten from a sleeping mother cat. As sand and rocks pelted the corpse, the soul snuggled safely in the grasp of light, and all the physical surrounding faded away.

The angel fulfilled its final duty to bring the soul through to the next dimension and released Anthony into the presence of their Loving God.

The last words of Anthony, the ones choked in prayer, had its conclusion. Anthony shouted, "AMEN!"

Those words did not stay with Anthony or float around somewhere. The words carried urgency, a plea before death.

The Everywhere-present God answered it immediately. The Sovereign God ordered a message and a new task to be carried out on earth as it was heard in heaven.

The Bishop's Business

Bishop Athanasius sent Marcarius and Amatas to find Anthony. They searched for days between sandstorms. After they reported they could not find a body, they all concluded that the desert buried the monk.

Athanasius sent messages to churches concerning Anthony's death. He then arranged a gathering at the large church in Alexandria to honor his deceased friend.

The stone building filled with a crowd of Coptic monks and old acquaintances, all younger than Anthony—younger by decades. The domed structure protected the mourners from the summer sun of Epip, Rome's July to August.

Before the rituals began, the elderly bishop overheard a young priest casually remark, "Anthony? Well, he was a good brother."

Athanasius stood with other respected clergy throughout the ceremony and prayers. He kept clenching his right fist around a stone-bead cluster in his palm. It emitted a quiet grinding sound. When his hand relaxed, he moved his fingers over the smoothed pebbles, revealing his prayer beads and a small silver cross that dangled from its tip.

Ceremonies and rituals led to long prayers and even longer liturgies that highlighted hope for a future resurrection. Finally, there was a dismissal of the gathering.

"The peace of God be with you. Go in peace. Amen."

As the congregation filed out, Athanasius gathered a few of his close friends, all of them bishops, to a small side structure covered with palm thatch. The setting was Romanesque, for it served as a place for quick discussions out of the sun. Minor to momentous decisions came from the talks that bounced around in the shade under palm branches.

Athanasius signaled that it would be a short—concise—talk. He started it with a sober lament.

"Anthony, our oldest friend—maybe the oldest man we knew—gave the Coptic Church the gift of praying with beads in our hands. You know how these help us pray longer. He taught us much. Anthony was a great brother."

The sky turned pale and tan. The sun dimmed because of high-flying dust. From the south, another *khamsin* threatened the city. Athanasius nodded his head to the group. The men had duties to attend to before the storm hit, and he had already made them late. He gave them a charge for the next year.

"Our church will remember him as 'Saint Anthony, the Great'—our first Desert Father. Our Everlasting God will move Anthony's gift beyond this time. His prayers live."

FURIOUS WINDS

Weather Report

Shelf cloud: A low, horizontal wedge-shaped cloud associated with a thunderstorm front. The underside of it often appears turbulent, boiling, and wind-torn. It can take up the whole horizon.

Wall cloud: These compact storm clouds range from a fraction of a mile up to nearly five miles (8 km) in diameter. Many wall clouds exhibit rapid upward motion and cyclonic rotation.

Funnel cloud: A funnel cloud becomes a tornado when it comes in contact with the ground. Tornadoes have destructive wind speeds from 100 miles per hour (160 kph) to more than 300 miles per hour (480 kph).

Gathering Clouds

January 2015

Cold outside. Grey skies. Windy.

His is the only silver-haired head, the only grey-beard of the top floor and special-tech wing of the bank's corporate headquarters. He quickly jerks straight in his chair.

Don't look asleep. Don't give in to sleep.

His motion looks like he received a shock through his keyboard. Now his heavy fingers tap and clack to match and join the same sounds heard throughout the cube farm; music to managers' ears.

In front of him, beside one of the two desktop monitors, are documents clipped to a copyholder stand. These have not shifted for over an hour.

"Steve. Got that spreadsheet for me? Want it by noon."

You're barking at a contractor hired to compose word directives not design a busy-work numbers page. Analytics for the anal retentive. It'd be in your hand if finished. 'No.' Now go away.

"I'm sorry. Not yet. Soon."

February

Precision climate control. Defused fluorescent lighting. White noise.

The artificial environments muffle, muzzle, and blind. They make his eyes want to close. Time for the usual afternoon fight against sleep—the signal for more breakroom coffee.

More bad coffee. More trips to the men's room. Living prostate and bladder commercial here.

His feet quick-step him to the restroom. He returns and notices how a few pages of piled memos obscure the desk phone, yet the blinking message light emits a rhythmic glow reflected on the desk's surface. He pokes the numbers for voicemail to discover the time-sensitive message is six hours old.

The message: "So, give me a call, like right now, so we can move forward." Click.

His own "right now" is a stare down at a pop-up message on the screen. It waves for attention: "Progress Report Meeting — Conference Rm 4A — 3 PM".

His sweaty hand drops the phone handset onto its cradle.

Almost ready.

March

Still cold. Not enough light. More wind.

His face, the oldest among the dozen expectant young ones, forces a smile to talk about procedure manuals.

Team lead—lead this young troop. Decades ago, led the charge in smoky mud huts of tropical Africa.

He begins his onboarding speech. "Welcome ... *blah-blah-blah* ... information ... *blah-blah-blah* ... and this video...."

Taught a tribe to read; write; understand God's Word in their language.

"We'll make it easier for agents to read, write, and publish. All digitized ... no paper ... all devices."

Sound throaty. No behest from the chest. Thin, not deep. Pitch all wrong. Volume an audible wobble. Awkward dance with words.

The young writers look more aloof than serious.

Then Liberia's civil war. Senseless war in Africa.

A seasoned co-worker takes her moment to start the video. He sits and stares at the projection on the wall that serves as a video screen; then at the window; out the window. Before the familiar ending and credits, he slinks out.

Get out! Got to get out!

He holds his arms close to his chest as if he wants to keep his body from throwing off an odor like the smell of a stale and forgotten sandwich on a plate in the employees' refrigerator.

Maybe dying. Get to the restroom. Restroom!

He pushes open the door.

Stop!! Women's restroom! No one here. No witnesses. Thank you, Jesus!

He spins toward the men's room.

Several heads turn and look up then back to their screens as he limps to his desk, weaving through the side aisle.

Seen! The lost look lost. Find the desk. Find a folder slot and the way out.

Lunch time. Alone. He sits in the sunlight and feels no warmth. It is filtered through the breakroom windows.

Back at the desk, he sees a pop-up message for another meeting.

Tell them brain injury. Bicycling accident. Hit by a truck and almost died. Maybe did die. This is walking dead; nine years dead.

Waiting in a third-floor conference room, he hears a co-worker say, "Your skin turned grey." She tears up like she could see the future.

She continues, "Get help. I'll call."

"No, don't call for an ambulance."

Go home early. Just need sleep.

Before he engages the car's clutch, he cries. Weeps.

Friday the 13th.

His first Friday unemployed. His head aches and ears ring.

Technical writing career over.

He takes a nap but wakes unrested. One word woke him. He heard it on the radio, read it on his computer screen, and friends voiced it to him. He repeats it as his eyes focus on—nothing.

"Disability."

Shelf Clouds

April

He reads—again—his favorite T.S. Eliot poem.

> *April is the cruelest month, breeding*
> *Lilacs out of the dead land, mixing*
> *Memory and desire, stirring*
> *Dull roots with spring rain....*
> *And I was frightened....*

He watches snow melt away from the brown grass that struggles toward green turf. The muddy flowerbed reveals puddles.

He won't smile; can't smile.

Told everyone it was a traumatic brain injury, "You know—a TBI thing."

He watches another streaming video about TBI and presses the pen hard onto the notepad to scribble the toll-free phone number. The video's young lawyer says, "So you should apply for Social Security Disability."

May

He reads the radiologist's note from the MRI results. "See," he brags. "They agree with me! It says, "minor shrinkage."

Now he walks with a cane to keep balance. He explains to all who ask, "Yes, I've fallen—forward. Walking or standing, sitting or lying down, it's like when you are in a Ferris wheel, and at the second it starts, you grab the safety bar. That's the panic I feel. And it's every moment! Even now."

June

The neuropsychologist's exam room at the University of Iowa Hospital and Clinics gets crowded with assistants and medical students. Late in the day, at the end of the eight hours of testing, Dr. Joe Barrash enters the examination room and sits at the table.

"Good news, Mr. Baker. You do not have a brain injury. Also, you are not a candidate for Parkinson's disease. Your brain is fine."

The doctor gestures around the room. His team nods with agreement.

"You scored well. Outstanding at times. That feared shrinkage of your brain? Normal for a man in his early sixties."

No. Not well. Must be something else, something terrible.

Dr. Barrash's voice, steady and soothing, continues. "You are in depression, Steve. We caught you before you dropped further down the dark well. You're on a ledge."

Another failure. Always fail. Hopeless.

"Doctor. I've told everyone that I have a Traumatic Brain Injury. What do I tell them now?"

"Tell them you have traumatic injury to your whole being," he replies. "Your soul, if you prefer."

Soul? A scientist talking about a soul? Yes, the soul can be injured. Yes, the soul hurts.

"If you have problems with your physical being, you go to a physician," says Dr. Barrash. "If you have problems with your mind, you go to a psychologist. If you have problems with your soul, you go to God. We can help you with the first two. You have resources for the third."

Permission. Permission from science—from neurology. Fix the brain. Seek God. Fix the soul.

Wall Cloud

July

Mom's Driveway
The summer's heat, the sun's brightness, Iowa's humidity. He talks with the social worker as Mom looks out the window at them.

"You have seen how dementia progresses. Has your family considered alternative care?"

Can't get her out. Can't be alone with this decision.

"And you, Steve? How are you coping? Depression is serious, especially for caregivers."

Not good. Oh no, tears.

"Fine."

Living Room
Home alone. Shallow breaths, rapid pulse, gut ache. Another attack. Forty minutes of snot and wailing.

August

Cool basement.
Dim lights and closed windows. The doorbell rings—again.

"Go away!" But no one hears. His cave absorbs sound.

His cell phone rings and the screen displays, "Dr. Ron."

"This report from Dr. Barrash recommends counseling. Do you know what kind you want?"

"Christian."

"There's an office in this building. We'll set you up."

Must be real. Need help. Getting help.

Counselor's Office

"I love God. I do." He squirms as his bladder fills and his hands sweat. Throat tightens.

Keep drinking water. Keep hydrated. Hold back the tears. Get through this.

"Steve, you need to grieve. Grieve your losses. You've lost much in your ministries. Then your jobs. Now your mom's dementia is taking her away. This week, acknowledge and grieve."

Going to be a tough week.

September

For the final straight mile of the bike trail, he clicks the bike's gearing, lifts off the saddle a bit, and sprints. The bicycle responds with the increase of stress through his legs.

Feel the burn. Alive to feel something. Bike up! White jersey, white helmet, white bike. Tom!

Tom signals as they fly past each other, so they both slow to circle back. They pull off to the grass and face each other, front wheel to front wheel.

They first banter with cycling talk then have a discussion about the deacon board's decision to help.

Tom says, "This is what churches should do. It's what we do. We help people through all kinds of trouble. Even illnesses—mental illness. Including yours as you fight depression."

Oh no, more tears. Throat's tight. Can't talk.

A few minutes later they orient their bikes back to their original directions. Simultaneously they press a foot to hook a shoe cleat into a pedal with a satisfying clack. Before they push off, Tom raises his voice for one last thought. He smiles, but his voice takes on thickness and strength. A prophet's pull of authority.

"Steve. Depression is ... your gift."

Funnel Cloud

October

Some gift! Worse with meds. Sleep, sex, vision all messed up!

The clinic calls, "Taper off this medication."

In the front of the house, he sits in a wrought iron chair under the glowing-red maple tree. In the living room, he has two chairs to choose from. The only time he leaves the house is to purchase some groceries and visit his mom.

Inside the house, he stands and looks through the big living room window to face the outdoors. He watches leaves blow off the trees and drift into rows beside the house.

Leaves are lucky. They're free.

November

Thursday

His vision is back to normal, and his nightly sleep resumes. Then the rebound from being off the drug begins.

Strange diarrhea. Not like bacterial or parasitical. Not like Africa or Mexico. Constant nervous poops. Losing weight.

Sunday

He sits in the worship center's theater seating, shifting his weight from one cheek to the other. He prays for the gift to go away.

Getting better. Must be. Maybe. Not sure. Amen.

He doesn't lift his head as the sermon begins.

What's with this talk about God caring for dead birds and flowers?

He whispers to Kathy that he is leaving, exiting early to avoid talking with people. She squeezes his hand as a signal that it's okay, but she presses her lips together and closes her eyes.

At home, he sees the phone's blinking message light.

Many calls. All from Mom. Listen later. Call later. Gotta rest. Gotta ride out this wave. Can't let Kathy see this meltdown.

Kathy returns home just as the landline phone rings again, but he picks up the handset before the phone's answering voice begins.

Mom's voice, "What day is today? Can't turn on the TV to find out. This medicine thing someone left here keeps beeping. Is this mine? Should I take the pills in this thing?"

"Mom, I'll be over … soon."

He listens to the stored messages. Each one, "What day is today? Can't turn on the TV to find out. This medicine thing someone left here keeps beeping."

December

Exam Room at the Clinic

He sits on the exam table with his shirt still unbuttoned. Kathy's hand rests on his shoulder.

"Mom must have fallen in the evening. I went over as soon as she called. I found her slumped against the wall in a chair by the phone. When I helped her get off the chair and then ready for bed, I could hear my pulse in my ears."

As his longtime friend and the nurse for his doctor, Sue speaks gently, slowly, and firmly. From her angle, she is at eye level but keeps her professional distance and stance as the head nurse in the clinic.

"Mr. Baker. From this moment on, you are not to take any responsibility to take care of your mom. Steve, you're blood pressure numbers right now are down from 186 over 105 when you called. It's now 168 over 96. You were to go to the Emergency Room because you were in a hypertension crisis. If it spikes like that again…."

She pauses to move her eyes to Kathy at Steve's side.

"You will have to take him to the ER."

Steve drops his gaze from the nurse and stares at the floor. He sees his feet dangling as he remains motionless on the exam table.

Insurance doesn't cover ER. More debt.

"Okay. But, my mom…"

Sue interrupts and speaks again to Kathy. She lifts a hand with her palm outward. "Get others involved. Take him home to rest."

Fellowship Hall at Church

It is the Sunday before Christmas Day. He stops speaking in mid-sentence and braces himself against a table loaded with Christmas pastries. Then, whoever he was talking to sees him shuffle away, each foot sliding on the floor. He moves in a straight line toward the door, pausing to let people with paper plates of sweets pass by. The crowd is cheerful, but his face is blank—no expression.

Walking dead.

He stops at an exit door as one of the church elders greets him.

"I'm not doing well. Going home. Find Kathy and let her know. She'll get ride home."

Basement at Home

He is comfortable in the dark. The heat from the space heater blowing over him warms his blanket as he binge-watches anything with time travel, especially *Doctor Who*.

Escape this ... universe.

WIND CHILL

Weather Report

Wind Chill: In the frigid winters of the North American and Canadian prairies, increased wind speeds accelerate heat loss from exposed skin. The measured effect is called the wind chill factor. The actual outside temperature may be 0°F (-17°C), but with a wind speed of 20 miles per hour (32 kph), to the skin it feels like -22°F (-30°C).

Frosted

Iowa's winter dry is arctic-air nose-bleed dry. The man walking in sub-zero wind rescues his nose with a scarf that also traps moisture for his sinuses. The outer surface of the scarf stiffens with fine ice crystals at the spot where warm exhales create a white badge of frost.

It's January again. Ghastly cold. The afternoon daylight dims as the sun arcs. It sets more in the south than the west. The high-flying ice crystals in the air act like little prisms in the sunlight to display rare afternoon sundogs. As his breath steadies in a cadence with his legs' pace, he successfully keeps the warmth he gained in the public library.

He pulls the wool wrap down a bit so he can see the patches of ice and snow on the city sidewalk. The dark polarized sunglasses protect his eyes from winter's harsh reflections, but they also obscure his path by frosting over as vapor escapes from behind the scarf. He moves them up off his nose a bit.

Almost home. Another quarter mile. Didn't think this through.

An hour before, he angled his first quarter-mile walk northeast to the pharmacy. The young woman in a white lab smock stopped smiling as she pronounced his blood pressure numbers.

"176 over 100. Does your doctor know this?"

"Yes. I should go home."

He didn't go home. The wind pushed him southeast to the library.

Blood pressure checked. Professionally. Documented. Walk home's gonna be painful.

Frozen

His earmuffs filter the squeaky sound of sub-zero snowpack under his boots. He hears his pulse. Because the broad-rimmed leather hat swirls wind away from his face, the exposed skin of his forehead does not sting from the wind-chill. He wears the sunglasses not so much for the sunlight but to keep his eyeballs from freezing. Frost forms on his eyelashes. His eyes keep tearing up.

His hand tires from holding the book he checked out. It was too big to fit in his coat pocket, and he didn't want to wedge it under his arm and trap his hand to his side. He keeps his balance with both arms out away from his body. He walks like a penguin over stretches of ice glazing the sidewalks.

Hope. Hope. Where's hope?

He looks up and notices the houses and how the exhaust belching from chimney stacks are white wisps not so much smoky but steamy, angling up and blowing south. He sees his house.

Another hundred yards. Zach Bass from "Man in the Wilderness" or "Nanook of the North." Not!

He pivots left a bit as a gap of sunlight shines through a street intersection. As he faces the street, from his right side, a school bus rumbles by. He completes his turn and puts his back to the wind.

Bus empty. Void of young souls.

He sees his shadow cast all bumpy-looking on the snow that had been scooped by a snowplow.

If there were children on the bus, what would they have seen if they looked out the windows? A sad old man wearing an Aussie hat.

A movie of himself—a documentary or a docudrama—clicks, and rattles in his mind as if it was an old 16-millimeter film projector, like one from his grade school days. The film projected in his mind is like a contemporary drone—shot looking down and flying upward. He is the figure in focus, but as the drone gains altitude, the hat and coat shrink to a darkened spot in the corner of the widescreen which brightens white as the snow swallows him, erases him. The disassociation ends when he enters his house.

Thawed

The kitchen. The stove and hot chocolate. More sugar.

He places the book down on the kitchen table next to his tablet that glows with a page of Scripture. Dr. Andrew Newberg's book, *How God Changes Your Brain*, invites him to read—like right now.

He retreats to a chair with the tablet and book in one hand and something hot in the other. He cuts off the radio with a remote control after he hears how low and dangerous today's wind chill is.

Bone-chilling cold. Brain-freezing cold. Chill down to the soul.

His soul had already turned cold. Frozen. An iceberg soul.

He opens the book like it was an award for braving frostbite. Where his thumb grabs the book, it opens to page 43. He holds it; it holds him.

Someone had highlighted the phrase, THE "GOD" CIRCUITS IN YOUR BRAIN.

A word forms in his mind. It was not the same word that carried him from the library to his front steps. That word "Hope" gave way to another word. He remembers it months after it was first tossed to him.

His urge to pushback and silence the word melts with another sip of the hot drink. The icicles caging his soul soften and thaw a bit as he stares at the book's subtitle: *Breakthrough Findings from a Leading Neuroscientist.*

He reaches for the tablet. Its screen glows with the online Bible, and his finger touches the screen at Joshua 1:8.

This Book of the Law shall not depart from your mouth, but you shall meditate on it day and night....

He tightens his grip on both the book and tablet to accept that one word he had refused to speak but now jumps out of his mouth.

"Gift."

GENTLE BREEZES

Coffee house air is not dry. The humidity from the brewing steams swirl like vapes in the room producing whiffs from coffee beans roasted then custom grounded and brewed. It is warm in the spacious restaurant that is mostly a coffee shop, but outside the spring winds of April move the leafless tree branches.

The university students and insurance agents keep their laptop computers open. Some students compose their assignments by gently tapping on keyboards while a few others are lost in their smartphones. Most of the coffee house patrons engage in caffeinated conversation.

Two men, an older bearded man and a young Emergency Medical Technician, sit on bar stools at a raised table by large windows that filter the late morning sun. These two friends had decided to spend Good Friday sipping java. One had that day off, and the other enjoys the perks of being a senior.

Blake says, "You look good, Steve. You don't look like you've put on any pounds this winter." Then he continues with his recount of life since January, but his gaze does not rise above the coffee mugs on the table. He mentions the switch in a prescription for psychotropic medication.

Steve lifts a cup to his lips and conveniently stares at Blake.

Going on five years now, friend. Depression at 35 is killing your soul. There's something else.

Steve responds to Blake's question. "My four months? Make it four years. 2015 was my year of darkness. 2016 began the year of hope. 2017, my year of confidence—I seriously started my book. 2018, courage. Went on a humanitarian mission trip for two weeks last summer—to Russia."

Blake lifts his face upward.

"Why? I mean, how? You were a mess. What happened?

Steve leans forward to speak quietly, yet the surrounding buzz of conversations does not overpower the calmness in his voice.

"You and I both know depression. We've both been on meds. But have you tried meditation?"

Blake squinches one side of the face.

Familiar look. Different churches but the same teachings; same conservative church pre-judging.

Then Steve sharpens the description, "Meditation with prayer beads."

Blake tightens his lips as his hand presses steady on his near-empty mug, keeping one eye open as if to say, 'Gotta leave soon.'

Steve pulls a small pouch from his pocket.

"I received something I can call a gift. Sent over 1600 years ago. It was forged in pain."

As an hour passes with a couple of restroom breaks for both of them, the coffee shop fills with a lunch crowd.

Blake pulls on his jacket. "I'll have my brain talk to God. Nutrition, exercise—and meditation. I need hope. And confidence. And courage. Help me get through the process."

"*Brain-talk Meets God-talk*. God woos us with his character. Rewire your brain and restore your peace. I'll email stuff to you, and you can borrow these beads."

He slides the pouch to Blake and says, "Remember, it's in present tense. 'He restores my soul.'"

PART 2

REWIRE AND RECOVER

BEGIN HERE

Trauma to the Body, Mind, and Soul

Depression is an illness of the brain. Its symptoms may appear as emotional because the offended mind and traumatized brain send their radicles deep to the soul. They damage the soul. That's why a person appears discouraged or sad, but those emotions are only symptoms of hurts the soul endures.

The soul in pain sends infectious messages back to the brain. Then like a virus, it changes the way the brain should function. Psychologists and counselors rightly call depression a mental illness.

"A sad soul can kill quicker than a germ," wrote John Steinbeck. That "germ" kills the vitality of any human being who experiences depression.

Rather than write my sad stories (and how I was set free from "sadness"), I offer to you, for these next few days, a gift in the guise of a book. Here begins a journey out of your storm stories if you seize this new method to cultivate hope.

There is hope here, and it will conquer depression.

You, who fight against depression, seem to get beat up by it no matter how hard you pray or how diligent you may be to memorize Bible verses. You struggle to keep good thoughts about God, but you mess that up, too. But here in this book is good news for you.

God will assist you to change your thoughts that will change your brain, and in that process, God works to restore your soul. It is God who created the soul, therefore he provides what is necessary to heal and restore your soul.

Part 1 of *Brain-talk Meets God-talk* (that you read or will read) is the story telling part. These provided an entertaining way to relay the research and background in the development of this book.

Part 2 lays out the principles of neurology and some theology for rewiring your brain with the truth your brain processes and what your soul craves. As you step all the way through Part 2, God will be at work to heal and restore you soul.

Before You Start

Brain-talk Meets God-talk meditation requires the use of a tactile stimulation tool. Tactile sensory stimulation involves the sense of touch, particularly through the fingers. The tool of choice is a set of Anglican (protestant) prayer beads.

The bead set is nothing more than a tool which happens to be a perfect configuration for organizing the content and controlling the time for meditation.

You will need the set of beads by Step 4, Dig In. You can find good resources to purchase beads online through eBay or Amazon, or from FullCircleBeads.com. If you have beads custom made, insist that the bead maker adhere to the pattern of 33 beads and a cross.

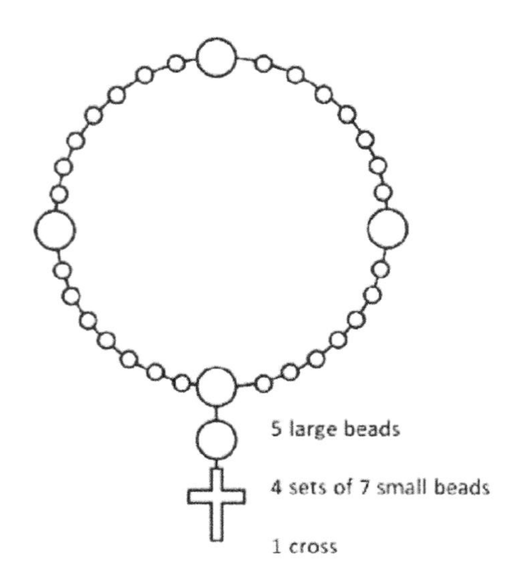

Brain-talk is *of* the brain. God-talk is *with* the brain. Tactile stimulation is sensed *by* the brain. Your brain is the battlefield for victory over depression.

Here are the steps taught in this book to achieve that victory.

Dig Around (Step 1)

When you receive a professional's diagnosis (as I did) of clinical depression, or you realize on your own that your mental disposition is more than sadness but a serious lack of vitality, it's time for some self-analysis and reflection. When you accept the reality that something is wrong, you then can do something about it. Unless you name the problem, you can't deal with it.

Dig Around describes depression. It gives you examples of behavior that may describe you and presents to you what may be wrong. It also introduces something that will prepare you for Step 2, Dig Out.

Dig Out (Step 2)

Your digging around pays off, but you need to be familiar with this book's terminology and tools: Brain-talk (neurology) and God-talk (theology).

You will learn a basic lesson from neurology to know what is going in your brain. Added to that is a friendly introduction to the theology of our Triune God's attributes (his oneness in three persons and his characteristics). The merging of the two "talks" is the reason for this book's title.

The information is basic and brief. This is not a study book on either science or theology but a practical manual that quickly educates you. Once your mind is ready, you will be prepared for Step 3, Dig Straight.

Dig Straight (Step 3)

This is a "to do" list to get ready to Dig In. It contains advice on where and how to make the most of your meditation time. You will master these simple instructions in one sitting.

Dig In (Step 4)

This begins the gift. Digging in is not simply sweeping clean the tangled mess of contradictions in the brain; it's discovering how proper neuroscience rewires your brain.

The gift enlarges as you see your personal value to God. After what your body, mind, and soul have been through, you will be given a method to enjoy the presence of God as he ministers to your body, mind, and soul. You will then be prepared for Dig Deep.

Dig Deep (Step 5)

This is the final step, but you will use it for the next 36 days. The 18 meditation exercises (twice repeated), which if practiced consistently every day, will begin to lift you from darkness, despondency, and depression. Your brain and God will be at work to apply what you meditate on. It takes about 20 minutes a day every day for at least three weeks as the brain adapts to new neurological habits. During that time, God is active to heal the deepest wounds of your soul.

Before you see yourself pulled from the dark depths of depression, it is necessary to recognize the face of depression. This may be a bit uncomfortable, but if this is your problem, let me help you embrace reality. If you don't identify and name the problem, you can't seek help to solve it.

It's time to start. Let's begin.

Flip the page to **Step 1, Dig Around**.

STEP 1: DIG AROUND

Depression Disrupts Life

Severe weather and storms disrupt life and property, but afterwards there is time to assess the damage. You poke and prod through debris and find a few things that didn't blow away in the tornado or float away in the flood waters. You simply dig around with hope to discover that all is not lost, but your world is rocked. Nothing really looks good. You see it through different circumstances, even in a different state of mind.

Depression is an altered state of consciousness about reality. It's not a feeling. It's beyond discouragement. Discouragement is a feeling, but hopelessness and despair are not feelings. These altered states of mind often come from physical and mental traumas to the brain, and the brain then fails to adapt to new circumstances. The mental pain, even self-loathing, follows to heighten the trauma to the brain. Then beyond mental anguish, these injuries and traumas affect the soul.

Just as disappointment relates to discouragement, hopelessness links to despair. Discouragement can pass away with a change of emotions. Hopelessness is like a brain-filter that creates a mindset that interprets life to say, "It's all hopeless and the circumstances will never be favorable for a happier life."

Hopelessness is also the sense of foreboding. It can lead you to believe that there will be no knock at your door with offers to help you. But worse is despair.

Despair causes you to assume that not only will there be no knock at the door, whatever is outside the door is probably something very bad. Then the brain signals the soul to hide, to disappear, because life is not worth living. The next dangerous step after despair is to find a final exit from life.

Depression Distorts Life

"With all the bad things happening, and I'm part of life's problems, I figured that perhaps the best thing for me was to be eliminated from the equation," said my friend who almost took his life.

This is the seriousness of depression that Christians are subject to, just like everyone else on the planet. Not all depression disorders bend a brain toward suicide, but the depressed life can take on an appearance that life is not worth living. Without getting help, the person afflicted with depression may look and act like this over an extended time:

Not showering/bathing — Not shaving/grooming
Lack of dental hygiene — Lack of clean clothes
Taking frequent naps — Tired all the time
Can't poop — Nervous poops
Oversleeping — Sleeplessness at night
Compulsively picking skin, hair, nose, ears
Avoiding loved ones — Loneliness
Low sex drive — Erratic sex drive
Emotionally extreme — Emotionally flat
Flaking on plans — Low confidence
Wasting time — Obsessed with guilt about wasting time
Brain fog — Poor concentration
Anger and angry at everything—angry at nothing;
Constant sense of guilt:

"I have done bad things."

Constant sense of shame:

"I am a bad person."

"I am a bad parent (son/daughter; brother/sister; husband/wife)";

Disassociation from thoughts, memories, surroundings, friends, and family;

Not knowing when or where will be the next time for a meltdown—and cry.

If you recognize a few of these observable symptoms in your life, it doesn't mean you are burdened with major depression. But if you identify with half or more of these outward symptoms of depression, likely you are in the agony of a depressive disorder and you need help. But you probably already know that.

The Statistics

The National Network of Depression Centers (nndc.org) posted these statistics:

- $210.5 BILLION lost earnings per year due to serious mental illness
- Depression is the leading cause of disability in the United States among people ages 15–44.
- Depression ranks among the top 3 workplace issues in the United States, along with family crisis and stress.
- 80% of those treated for depression show an improvement within four to six weeks of starting treatment.
- Two thirds of people with depression do not actively seek nor receive proper treatment.

There may be tears coming to your eyes as you reflect on your hurts. You have been injured and traumatized, and not only is your brain responding, your soul holds onto the hurts. It's agony. It's a human condition. Christians are subject to anguish and anxiety just like non-Christians.

Canadian conference speaker Brett Ullman correctly identifies how Christians struggle with depression. He relates his experience as a Christian church leader in the grips of that lonely and dark world. In a video, he calls Christians in churches who suffer from depression the "Walking Wounded".

There are times you want your brain to shut up and even shut down. Your brain stores the memories, and that's what's killing you. If you could, you would physically grab your brain through your skull and get it aligned to a better standard to make sense of your life's puzzle.

What the brain will do with memories and how it treasures them and brings them together with promptings, as though it wants to align a design for your life's meaning, may not be in the best interest of the soul. Repeated horrific thoughts convince the soul that life is and always will be horrifying. The negative cycle continues, but the brain does not want to stop its task to assemble memories to make some meaningful mosaic. It will continue on a dark path whether you want it or not.

Depression Disfigures Responses

What your brain does not need is a scolding, a sermon, or a sincere but wholly misguided diagnosis of a spiritual problem. It's hard to move forward in healing when you hear:

"Jesus makes you happy. Maybe you don't know Jesus."

"Maybe you need to pray more ... read the Bible more ... memorize a Bible verse."

"Be anxious for nothing. Stop disobeying God."

Depression is a mental disorder that requires trained professionals to diagnose and to help find treatments. It is not a problem of disobedience to God but an indication that something is malfunctioning in the brain.

Depression Distorts Truth about God

Rev. A.W. Tozer wrote, "What comes into our minds when we think about God is the most important thing about us."

Many of our thoughts about God are memories. We retain memories in our brains about God (or how God has been presented to us) which generously contribute to our logic and feelings. If we don't consciously curb the way we let our brains process memories, our feelings take charge over logic. Christians in depression have trouble with how they feel about God rather than how they rationally think about God.

I gathered the following list of truths (God's attributes) with contradicting lies from conversations with friends who suffered depression.

- Truth that God is All-knowing: God knows all things—the past, present, and future.
  Distortion and Lie: God lost track of me in the details of the universe.
- Truth that God is everywhere-present: God is everywhere in the universe.
  Distortion and Lie: Where was God when I needed him?
- Truth that God is All-powerful: God has all power because God *is* the only all-powerful being in the universe.
  Distortion and Lie: God may be all-powerful, but he doesn't use it to stop bad things from happening to me?
- Truth that God is Love: God does not simply love or act lovingly, God is pure love.
- *Distortion and Lie: God has fallen out of love with me.*
- Truth that God is good: God is good in all his intentions, motives, and actions.
  Distortion and Lie: With all the evil allowed in the world, God doesn't seem to be doing good to help my situation.
- Truth that God is Holy: God is pure in his character and is absolutely separate from sin.
  Distortion and Lie: I feel so guilty and ashamed that God must be very disappointed with me.

There are times when you feel you cannot trust God because your brain keeps bringing up twisted memories and distortions about what God is like. Let me confess. This was my problem. This contributed to my depression.

Depression Connects the Wrong Dots

As a boy, I enjoyed the *Connect the Dots* games and puzzles. It was the best way I knew, except for *Color by Number*, to draw good pictures. The rest of my artwork looked awful. But for more fun, I learned how to distort pictures by purposefully connecting the dots out of order. Maybe it appeared that I was trying to imitate Picasso because my drawings had people and animals with odd-shaped noses and eyes. Also, I seemed to be the only one amused with that technique!

I did something similar the day my family visited the Des Moines Botanical Center. It was one of my "good" days, but I did tire of wandering around all the plant life, so I sat at a table of crayons and coloring pictures. A picture of a bucket with flowers became my project to color, and I applied my talent to distort.

I turned the drawing upside down and then created this face with a flowerpot hat. It looks a bit insane, but I smiled as I showed it to my wife.

I rarely laughed in those days, so that's why she kept it on our refrigerator as a reminder of a brighter day during my darker times.

But it is a dangerous practice to warp theological concepts by turning truth upside down, inside out, and sideways—and believing them! A person in depression can move from seeing God as beautiful to God as frightful.

I didn't perceive that until I read *The God-Shaped Brain* by Dr. Timothy Jennings. The book helped me realize that I held subconscious and dark depictions of God. I knew better, but my sickness led my thoughts about God down dark pathways to murky places. Digging around those dark places brought out the need for a mind-change.

Brain-talk Meets God-talk was conceived while I was in the dark, but there were moments of light and truth to help me.

Prepare to Dig Around

Allow God to meet you in your pain; not just physical pain, but mental distress.

"In the presence of God—Father, Son, and Holy Spirit." This declaration will be your banner that God is already with you, ready for your logical and emotional responses.

Starting today, and through the next 36 days, invite the Trinity into your presence and pain. It is up to God how he handles it, but this you may expect of God: He promised to be with you no matter what level of pain or darkness that engulfs your mind.

You can start today by learning how to correctly breathe.

Diaphragmatic Breathing

This is not yoga. This is not a New Age mystical practice.

Deep breathing is biologically needed and mentally therapeutic. God designed us to breathe deeply. Deep breathing triggers neurological responses to the brain's frontal lobe—it calms your mind.

Breathing through the nose increases the release of nitric oxide, improving the function of the lungs. If you do not have a habit to breathe from your diaphragm, known as diaphragmatic breathing, your muscles need to be strengthened.

During your meditation sessions, do your best to slowly take in each breath through your nose to extend your belly. Sinus troubles that force you to mouth-breathe should not hinder you from deep breathing. Just tighten the aperture of your lips to slow down the inhales and exhales. Because you will be in a private area, you may want to release the belt buckle of your trousers, even unsnap tight clothing if you aren't wearing a loose-fitting outfit.

Your diaphragm needs room to expand downward, and your lungs require freedom to push outward. Try this exercise:

Take a large phone book (or a couple of medium weight books) and place it on your tummy below your rib cage as you lie down on your back. Focus on your breathing to change the way you breathe by raising the book with only your lungs.

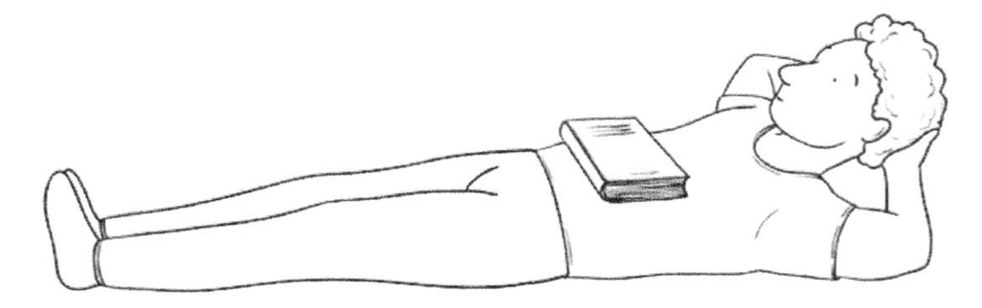

- Lift the book up about 1 inch (2–3 cm).
- Relax to exhale. The book will go down when you relax.
- Breathe in with only your diaphragm but don't let your rib cage expand as you inhale.
- Repeat this breathing exercise for about 3–5 minutes.

The more often you do this, the more your brain connects the purposeful breathing to your meditation routine. It will soon be a good habit.

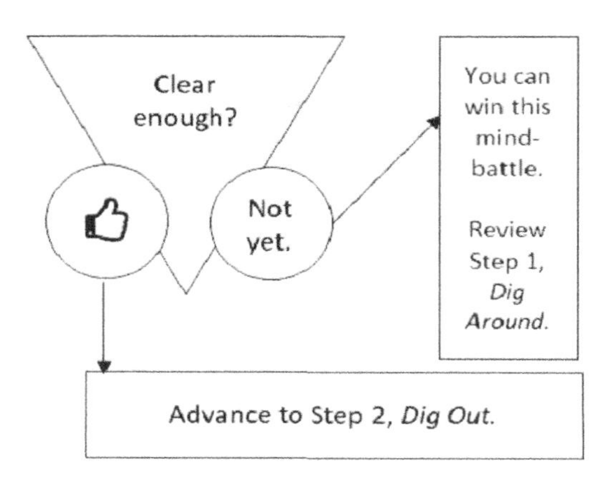

STEP 2: DIG OUT

Dig Out with Brain-talk

This is about neurology as Brain-talk. This book aims to lead you toward mental wellbeing and to enjoy the serenity of the mind. But it is necessary to have your brain trained to re-wire. Neurologists refer to such re-wiring as neuroplasticity.

This section should not bog you down for hours. It introduces you to only enough brain science before it brings up theology.

There are a couple of functions of the brain to understand, so when you meditate, know that you aren't doing anything that is harmful. When you start to see improvements in your mental health, it is because you have purposefully re-wired your brain's function for healthy thinking.

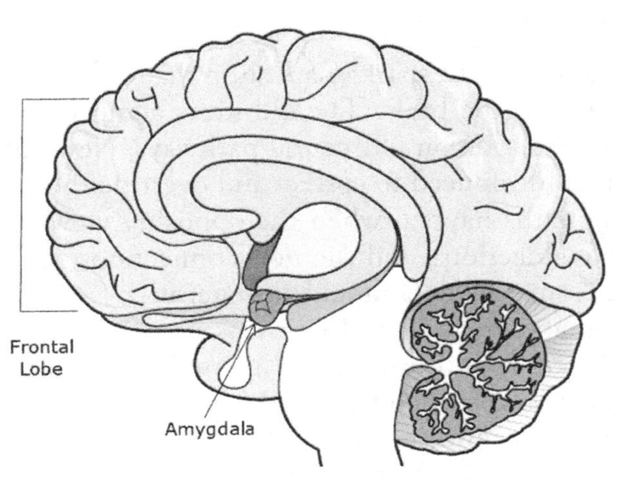

Brain-talk: Serenity vs. Anxiety

The Brain's Amygdala

The amygdala is a small, almond-shaped piece in the physical center of your brain. It is the center that processes anxiety, fear, and anger. It also inhibits the logic processes in the frontal lobe. It signals to your adrenal glands to pump adrenaline for FIGHT or FLIGHT or FREEZE when responding to danger. It also tells your body to produce cortisol, the stress hormone.

The Brain's Frontal Lobe

The frontal lobe function allows you to project future consequences resulting from your current actions. It's the part of your brain that lets you choose between the good and bad (or the better and best) action to take. It allows you to override and suppress poor social skills freely. You can determine similarities and differences as the frontal lobe gives you the power to use critical thinking to compare and contrast between things or events.

The Brain's Neural Pathways

Every thought ignites a spark of a neuron that communicates with different parts of the brain. The old ideas about God, like God doesn't love you, ride on old neural pathways. New and truthful ideas must be introduced to correct and override those old paths. New neural paths happen when the opposing views (the truth) create new connections, and the new connections activated over and over, become the default and stronger way.

Several years ago, I taught English as a second language (ESL) to adult refugees from Burma and Bhutan. My students could not remember new words when I spoke them only once or twice in our lessons. The curriculum encouraged teachers to provide many ways to repeat words for the language learners. Not only were students to repeat the words used in drills, examples, and homework, they had to "own" the words.

The neurological science applied in ESL lessons required creative ways to implement the words up to SEVENTY (70) times in one day in multiple situations and environments. By day's end, they would know the word, and their brains were ready to master the next set of English words.

The Brain's Neuroplasticity

The ESL students' brains were being re-wired to think in English because they developed new neural pathways in the language centers impressing their minds. Sparking neurons connected thoughts to other parts in their brains, and a neurological phenomenon happened every time they spoke and repeated new words.

Your brain changes for good or bad, for better or worse because of the way you respond to words. When new thoughts from words change the brain, this is neuroplasticity.

Dig Out with God-talk

The Attributes of God

The Bible gives us descriptions of God. It gives us clear insights into God's character. Theologians call a quality of God's nature an *attribute* (noun: A-truh-byoot). Attributes of God are eternal, infinite, and right. The truth of God's character should move our lives toward God. God woos us to with himself with his nature.

The word *attribute* (verb: uh-TRI-byoot) is something we do—to regard as resulting from a specific cause. "He attributed her bad mood to a headache. She attributed his accident to clumsiness."

We must not attribute to God anything that is not true. That is the easiest way to distort what God is like. Distortion moves our lives away from God.

C.S. Lewis said, "The heart cannot rejoice in what the mind rejects as false." When my mind presumed God to be like the human authorities in my life, including the ones who abused their power over me, I lost my heart's joy for obedience to God. I secretly believed, in the darkness of my mind, that God is like fallible human beings.

But by reviewing and meditating on God's attributes and how God profoundly loves me, I could step out of the darkness that characterized my depression.

It takes only one distortion of the truth, especially over a lifetime, to create distrust in the God who loves us. Not everyone tumbles into an altered reality of depression, but everyone knows what it is like to have joy ripped away because of lies told to them and lies said about them.

One of God's attributes is that he is truthful. He cannot lie. He cannot lie to me or lie about me. This truth liberated me.

Our Triune God

The Trinity is God the Father, the Son, and the Holy Spirit—One God in Three Persons.

I venture carefully to be faithful as I present the Trinity in this book. Saint Augustine of Hippo from the 5th century wrote a warning to those who would teach on the Trinity:

"Because in no other subject is error more dangerous, or inquiry more laborious, or the discovery of truth more profitable."

The Trinity is God's doctrine. God decided to reveal himself to humanity as three persons in one God. No other religion teaches it; no other faith could invent it. The doctrine of the Trinity is uniquely ours in Christianity.

Jesus' disciples had more to expand their understanding beyond monotheistic Judaism to accept Jesus as God, equal to the LORD (Yahweh) Father. In the intimate conversation Philip had with Jesus, he asks, "Lord, show us the Father...."

In reply, Jesus says, "Whoever has seen me has seen the Father."

Earlier Jesus said to a skeptical crowd, "I and the Father are one ... the Father is in me, and I am in the Father."

The effective use of the Trinity in this book is to declare that each person of the Trinity share God's attributes. Though each member of the Trinity has a specific ministry in our lives, each member of the Godhead is co-equal and co-eternal to the others in all known attributes. God is and acts as God in all three persons of the Trinity.

The Shield of the Trinity (in English) is an aid to understand this. Theologians of the 13th century drew it.

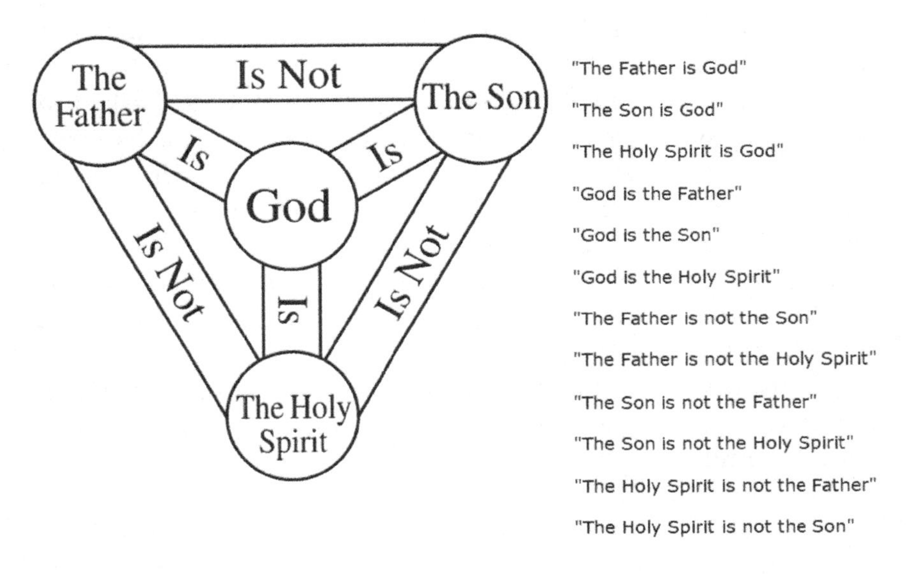

The meditation exercises presented in this book are worded in a Trinitarian frame. This is all part of the good God-talk to merge with active Brain-talk.

Merge Brain-talk with God-talk

Structured Brain-talk (neurology)
PLUS
Truthful God-talk (theology)
EQUALS
Biblical and Christian meditation.

Hebrew: to meditate is to *hagah*

The Semitic tribes were not known for raising dairy cows. So, I don't understand why so many Bible teachers use Joshua 1:8 to describe meditating, that it is like a cow chews cud. Nothing in the context of this passage suggests imitating bovines with their digestive systems. Besides, cows need more water than what the desert yields, so Israelites didn't use cows in their illustrations. Camels and sheep yes, but not cows.

The word for meditate in Joshua is *hagah*, which means to mutter.

Though I am from Iowa, I am not a farmer. I have asked my farmer friends who have vast knowledge in animal husbandry if they have ever heard a cow talk or communicate with a mutter. They all give me a strange look and then smile, getting ready for me to tell a joke.

Hagah is interpreted and applied only to human speech, because only humans who are created in the image of God on this planet can use spoken language.

Muttering is the language of pondering and meditating. To mutter is to speak words and sentences quietly. With the mouth. Audibly. Intellectually.

Meditation is softly spoken words at any time of the day or night with analytical and intellectual integrity. It is not just a regurgitation of Bible verses but the continual flow of thoughts from God's Word while contemplating the meaning and application of the words.

Also, meditating was God's command to Joshua and the tribes of Israel. Meditating is a command that can be applied to Christians.

Greek: to think is to *logizomai.*

In the New Testament, the Apostle Paul tells the believers in Philippi that they are to *logizomai*—to think. They are to think on that which is true, honorable, just, pure, lovely, commendable, excellent, and worthy of praise.

We humans can think on these high levels and abstracts, but we also have minds that wander. Try thinking "God is good" for 20 minutes straight. You'll need some help after a couple of minutes.

Brain-talk Meets God-talk teaches you to meditate like a Hebrew while you think like a Greek but in your language.

You can now legitimately talk about meditation as both a neurological and theological activity. This is the merger of what your brain is designed to do with the concepts God reveals. He wants you to thoroughly think on the truth and the goodness of God.

And if you do "according to all that is written in it (The Book)," he promises good things for your life. That is why he encourages you to meditate and to be strong and courageous. You are not only allowed to contemplate, but you are also commanded to meditate.

You can do this.

Prepare to Dig Out

So be brave. And, right now, take a break and get some exercise.

It's time for a walk. Get your body moving and raise your heart rate. You don't have to run or walk fast (or in my case, limp fast). Exercise will complement meditation routines. They work together for good mental health. And while you are walking, you can pray.

Pray the Prayer of Abandonment

Ask God for clarity in the next step. Seek him for confidence. Ask him for courage.

Read Thomas Merton's *Prayer of Abandonment* all the way through. Reread it and pray it out loud. Write it out completely. Focus on this as your prayer to God today and tomorrow.

My Lord God,

I have no idea where I am going. I do not see the road ahead of me. I cannot know for certain where it will end. Nor do I really know myself, and that I think I am following your will does not mean I am actually doing so.

But I believe the desire to please you does in fact please you. And I hope I have that desire in all I am doing. I hope I will never do anything apart from that desire. And I know if I do this you will lead me by the right road though I may know nothing about it. I will trust you always though I may seem to be lost and in the shadow of death. I will not fear, for you will never leave me to face my perils alone.

Add Praise to Diaphragmatic Breathing

Claim back the God-given gift of life and breath. The Eastern religious practices hijacked deep breathing for their falsified contemplations. Add to your exhale a statement of praise as you practice breathing. Here's a favorite:

Because of the Cross, glory to God forever.

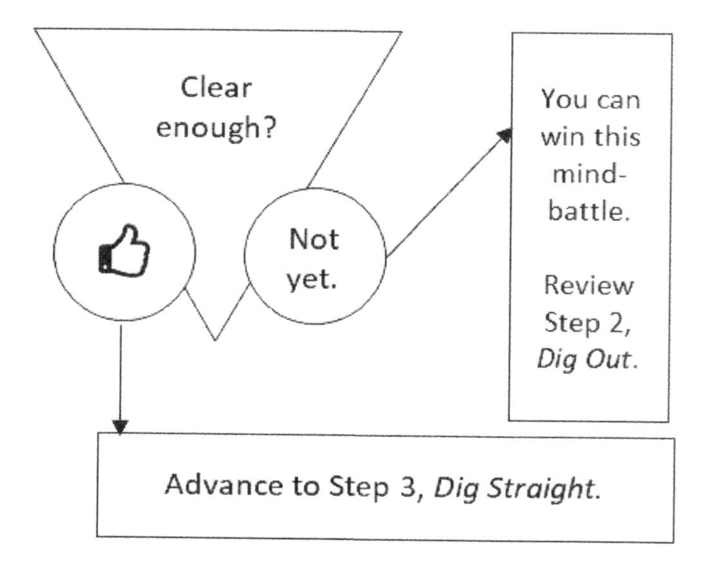

STEP 3: DIG STRAIGHT

Straight for Meditation—Not Memorization

The Daily Focus meditations of *Brain-talk Meets God-talk* are brief sessions of 15 to 20 minutes. Within that short time, you will softly speak Scriptural truths nearly 100 times.

The words you speak will build or reinforce new neural pathways in the brain to replace the uncomfortable thoughts you may retain about God. Your declarations of the truth override even the most deceptive lies your mind may have buried, especially the lies about God's love for you and his compassion toward you.

Meditation in this book is not the memorization of Scripture. The mental discipline the brain uses to memorize is not relaxing but demanding. Scripture memorization can give the brain a workout, and if you are in depression, you do not need more stress in the brain. Meditation is stress-free.

Straightforward Scripture

You are at liberty to use the same Daily Focus as many times as you want, but as you progress forward, discover how the attributes of God are purposefully listed in an order that logically moves you to the next one. The driving content for each Daily Focus that looks at God's attributes are the chosen Bible verses. They were interpreted and applied for *Brain-talk Meets God-talk*.

Some of the biblical texts are straightforward about what God says about God. Other Bible verses take a bit more study to discover God's personality, yet these also pull you closer to God's intention and direction for your mind. These all:

- Promote the truth about the known attributes of God;

- Protect your mind and soul as you rest in the presence of our Triune God;
- Point out the loving relationship God cherishes with you;
- Permit you to be quiet and focus on our Triune God who heals your soul, mind, and body.

Unplug from Distractions

Find a quiet place away from distractions. Silence or unplug your landline phone. You can silence or turn off your mobile devices, but you can also activate the "Do Not Disturb" mode on your smartphone and "Airplane Mode" for your tablet or iPad®. This is especially helpful if choose to read the Daily Focus meditations on an electronic device.

This is YOUR time with YOUR God. Do not let anyone hijack it from you.

You need twenty minutes without disturbances or distractions. The quietness allows you to hear your voice speak God's truth. If your living situation makes it difficult to find "alone time," consider using a chapel or a quiet room at your church.

Music?

You have the liberty to listen to soft instrumental music, but songs with words are distracting. Even instrumental music may have lyrics that trigger your memory. The words you subconsciously recall can interrupt the stanzas of truth from the Daily Focus. Good things can become the enemy of God's best thing. For meditation, the best is quietness. Wait until you finish meditation and then enjoy your favorite playlist.

Some "Don'ts"

Don't Slight the History

We Christians have a rich history of devotion to God. The early church fathers paid dearly to promote the faith. The Coptic monk Saint Anthony the Great was a courageous man who lived to 105 years of age. He introduced the concept of prayer beads for spiritual discipline over 1000 years before the Roman Catholic Church introduced the Rosary.

Anthony was not an ignorant man; he was quite intelligent. But he never learned to read or write. At 100 years old he refuted an errant priest who was teaching heresy about the Trinity. Perhaps he used a string of beads to keep his thoughts in order.

Don't Dis the Beads

Beads were never promoted as sacred objects to worship, therefore think of the beads as similar to a printed out prayer list or a fashionable silicone wristband that reminds you to pray.

There is nothing mystical about the prayer beads. Literature from the Anglican Church addresses this concern when, in the mid-1980s, the protestant denomination introduced prayer beads for private prayer and liturgical worship.

For meditation, the beads provide tactile stimulation, the soothing sensation through the fingers that your brain recognizes as a signal to breathe a diaphragmatic breath and quietly voice out the truth.

Continuous beads are, after all, not just a mode of representation of truth but also a means of concentration on truth. They represent a symbolic type of recollection. You breathe, and each bead reminds you to speak out the thought from the Daily Focus.

You recall. You think. Your voice and the tactile stimulation keep you on track.

You voice out the thought, and one thought moves to another with the same wording. The beads strung together and lightly pinched between your fingertips keep you paced and from losing your place. The last bead is a signal to stop.

Consciously moving your fingers from bead to bead prevents random or unconnected ideas. You won't bounce from this to that. The tool helps the mind to focus for twenty minutes, moment by moment.

Don't Miss the Poetry

I didn't compose rhyming verse, but I utilized a rhythm in the wording. I crafted the words so that a sentence could be broken apart and still hold a workable thought and yet stay true to English grammar. It's nothing near the skill of a master poet, but it provides a succinct expression of truth.

Prepare to Dig Straight

It is essential that you sit in a comfortable chair.

Be Still...

...in your seat: Sit in a chair that allows you to sit up straight in front of a table so you can see the open book. A small pillow behind your back will help you with your posture.

...in your upper body: Sit straight but not stiff. Allow the natural curve of your spine to be comfortable. Your head and shoulders should rest without effort on the top of your vertebrae.

...with your legs: Don't cross them. This impedes blood circulation. Let the bottoms of your feet touch the floor.

...with your arms and hands: The beads will lace in your fingers, and you can rest them on top of your legs.

...with your eyes: You need to see the pages of this book open to the Daily Focus, so arrange the book to be in front of you. You will eventually be able to close your eyes, but you need to return to the text with open eyes. Each time you begin a new stanza, you will need the book, so prop it up and secure the pages open with binder clips. If you read this book on your mobile device, angle it so you can see the screen.

Note: Closing your eyes will be comfortable, but it can make you almost too relaxed. The finger movements with the beads will remind you to breathe, look up when necessary, and keep your mind from wandering and falling asleep.

Regulate Your Deep Breathing

This helps calm your mind as well as enrich your body with oxygen.

During your meditation sessions, do your best to slowly take in each breath through your nose to extend your belly. After you speak the phrase, empty your lungs as much as possible when you exhale.

Enrich the Time

Do … not … hurry.

This is meditation. Don't rush it.

The session is most effective when you speak clearly and slowly. Completing three circles takes 15 to 20 minutes.

If unwanted thoughts intrude, acknowledge them and then let them go. Move on to the next bead and speak the truth.

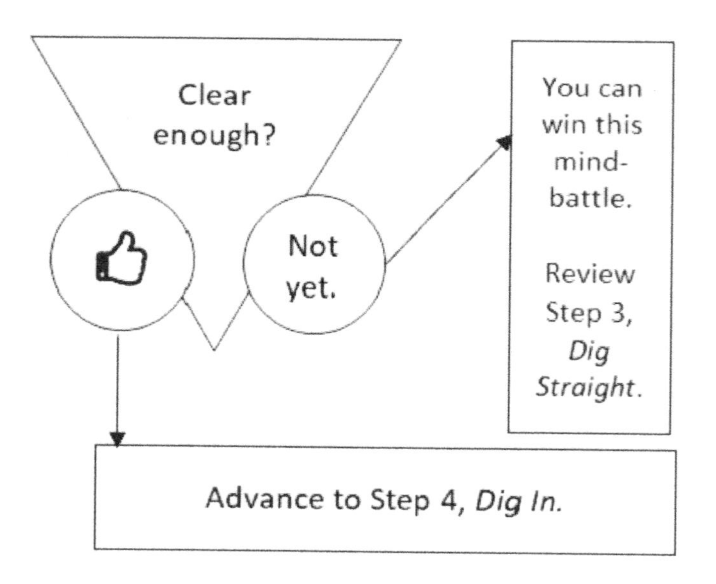

STEP 4: DIG IN

Quick Reference Guide

The Basic Lesson

1) When you have regulated your breathing, inhale and then read out loud the Scripture verse.

2) With the next breath, read out loud the Interpreted Truth. With another breath, read out loud the Applied Truth.

3) Hold the cross in your fingertips, inhale and then quietly praise God.

4) With the next inhale, move your fingers to the first large bead, and then quietly speak to acknowledge God's presence: "In the presence of God—Father, Son, and Holy Spirit."

5) Begin the first circle around the beads.

2 Chronicles 16:9 (NLT)

The eyes of the Lord search the whole earth in order to strengthen those whose hearts are fully committed to him.

God sees and searches the whole earth.

God sees and searches for me.

✝ Because of the Cross, glory to God forever.

● In the presence of God—**Father**, Son, and Holy Spirit.

● The Father sees and searches the whole earth.

⊗ Father sees and searches for me.

⊗ Father sees ⊗ and searches ⊗ for me.

● In the presence of God—Father, **Son**, and Holy Spirit.

● The Son sees and searches the whole earth.

⊗ Jesus sees and searches for me.

⊗ Jesus sees ⊗ and searches ⊗ for me.

● In the presence of God—Father, Son, and **Holy Spirit**.

● The Holy Spirit sees and searches the whole earth.

⊗ Holy Spirit sees and searches for me.

⊗ Holy Spirit sees ⊗ and searches ⊗ for me.

<u>First circle</u>:

Refer to the Father

<u>Second circle</u>:

Refer to the Son

<u>Third circle</u>:

Refer to the Holy Spirit

Assigned Meanings for the Beads

Begin Your Focus

✝ The **CROSS**

Inhale with a diaphragmatic breath, and then slowly exhale as you quietly acknowledge the truth of Christ's sacrificial death.

"Because of the Cross, glory to God forever."

Welcome the Trinity

● The **FIRST LARGE BEAD**

Inhale with a diaphragmatic breath, and then slowly exhale as you quietly acknowledge the presence of our Triune God.

"In the presence of God—Father, Son, and Holy Spirit."

Complete the Circles

● The **FOUR LARGER BEADS**

Inhale with a diaphragmatic breath, and then slowly exhale as you quietly affirm the INTERPRETED TRUTH. Declare the truth for a Person of the Trinity.

"The Father sees and searches the whole earth."

⊗ The **SMALLER BEADS** (four sets of seven)

Inhale with a diaphragmatic breath, and then slowly exhale as you quietly affirm the APPLIED TRUTH. Declare the truth for a Person of the Trinity.

"Father sees and searches for me."

Three Times Around

One each for the Father, the Son, and the Holy Spirit

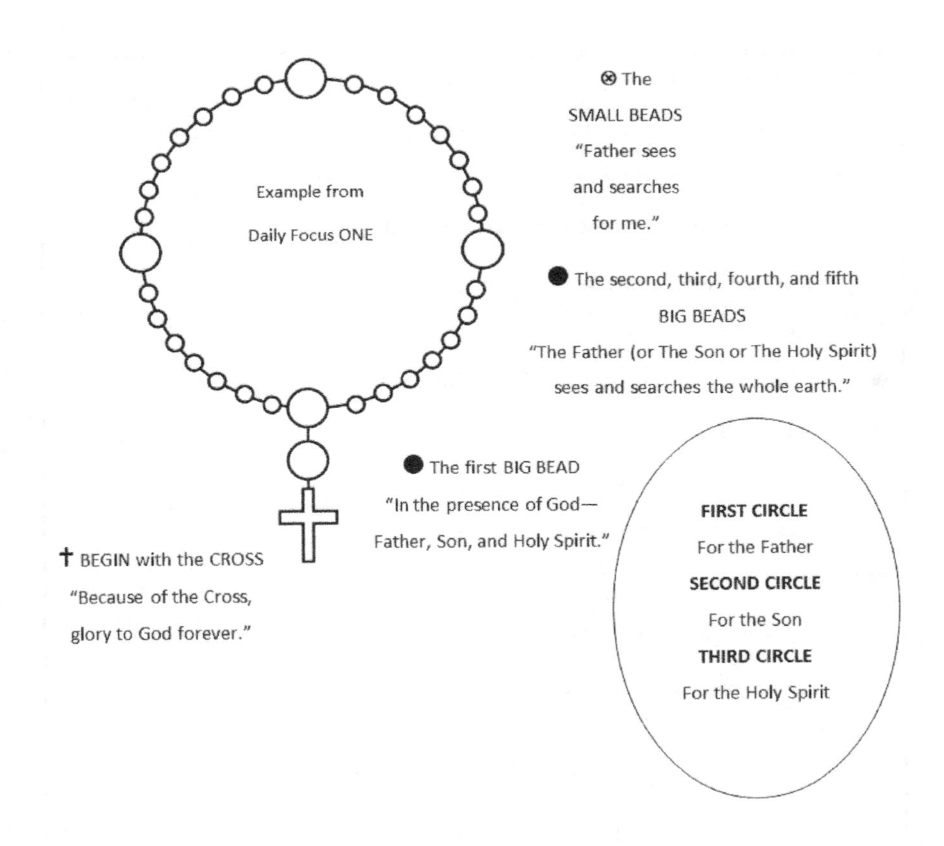

The Page in Front of You

This is what a Daily Focus looks like. Here is how to begin. With your beads in hand, you will make three circles around, one each for the Father, then the Son, then the Holy Spirit.

2 Chronicles 16:9 (NLT)

The eyes of the Lord search the whole earth in order to strengthen those whose hearts are fully committed to him.

God sees and searches the whole earth.

God sees and searches for me.

✝ Because of the Cross, glory to God forever.

● In the presence of God—**Father**, Son, and Holy Spirit.

● The Father sees and searches the whole earth.

⊗ Father sees and searches for me.

⊗ Father sees ⊗ and searches ⊗ for me.

● In the presence of God—Father, **Son**, and Holy Spirit.

● The Son sees and searches the whole earth.

⊗ Jesus sees and searches for me.

⊗ Jesus sees ⊗ and searches ⊗ for me.

● In the presence of God—Father, Son, and **Holy Spirit**.

● The Holy Spirit sees and searches the whole earth.

⊗ Holy Spirit sees and searches for me.

⊗ Holy Spirit sees ⊗ and searches ⊗ for me.

Prepare to Dig In

Maximize Your Breaths

Before you begin the rotation around the beads, take four or five slow, deep breaths. You don't have to count them if you touch the four tips of the cross with each inhale. After touching the fourth point, read the Scripture out loud.

Pull all the breaths you inhale with your diaphragm. Do not rush it. After each breath in, pause slightly then exhale. The deep breaths will keep you from starving for oxygen, and the pacing will prevent hyperventilation.

Yawn

There you go, you now must yawn. It's all right to yawn any time during the routine. It adds extra oxygen to your brain. Get it done and keep going.

Magnify the Worship

Think of meditation as your time to worship privately. It is your time alone with God. God enjoys your presence, so enjoy the separated time to know him intimately. The entire session (3 times around the circle of beads) takes 15 to 20 minutes. Our Immortal and Eternal God is in no rush with your fellowship.

Unwanted Thoughts

Acknowledge them and keep going. Move to the next bead and repeat the next stanza.

Too Relaxed

If the Daily Focus meditation rests you so that you feel sleepy before its conclusion, it means your brain is de-stressing. That's a good thing. Therefore, your finger movements will prompt you to the next bead. To keep alert, look at the Daily Focus page or take a glance at your beads as you move to the next word or phrase.

Break Apart the Stanzas

When you are half-way around the circle, speak out each word or word phrase with a separate bead. This allows your brain to deeply process the wording of each stanza.
⊗ Father sees ⊗ and searches ⊗ for me. ⊗ Father sees ⊗ and searches ⊗ for me.
For the seventh bead in the group, repeat the whole sentence without a break.
⊗ Father sees and searches for me.
Do — Not — Hurry

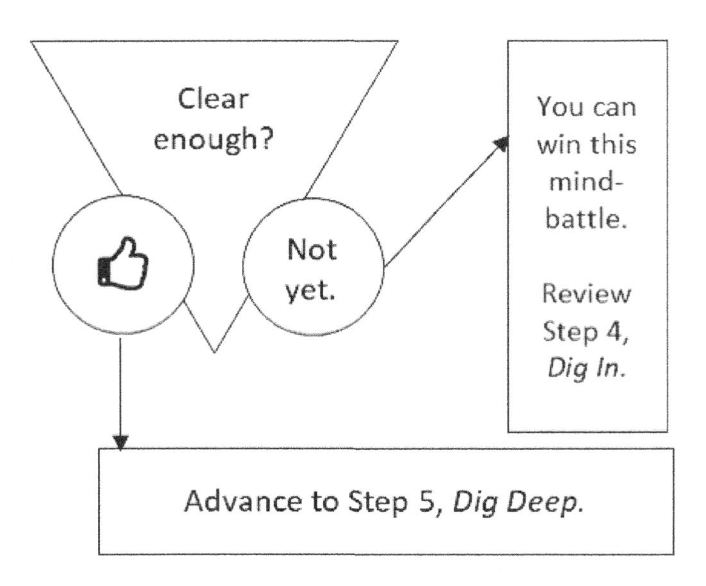

STEP 5: DIG DEEP

You have the liberty to choose two different ways to accomplish 36 consecutive days of Daily Focus meditation.

1. **Meditate with each Daily Focus two days in a row.**
   - Advantage: Your subconscious mind dwells on one attribute of God for two days, giving your mind time to process it longer before you proceed to another attribute presented in the next Daily Focus.
   - Example: Daily Focus ONE (All-knowing God) for your first day and the second day; Daily Focus TWO (Everywhere-present God) for your third day and the fourth day, etc.
2. **Meditate with a new Daily Focus each day.**

   If you meditate 18 consecutive days with a new Daily Focus, then repeat the routine for the next 18 days beginning with the first one.

   - Advantage: You will build your theological mindset faster. When you repeat the routine the second time, the characteristics of God will already be familiar to you.
   - Example: Daily Focus ONE for the first day, Daily Focus TWO for the second day, etc. After 18 days, then repeat Daily Focus ONE for the nineteenth day, Daily Focus TWO for the twentieth day, etc.

IMPORTANT: Arrange your time to meditate in consecutive days. The neurological process is better heightened without interrupting the days.

Before each Daily Focus, I include "Brain-talk in 100 Words". It's something to get your brain ready for that particular session. Nothing complicated; it relates to the day's topic.

The pages are designed so that you can use binder clips to keep the book open to both the Brain-talk in 100 Words page and the Daily Focus page.

It's time to begin. Dig deep.

ONE

GOD-TALK: ALL-KNOWING GOD

God knows all things—the past, the present, the future.

God's knowledge has no boundaries regarding time or space, so in every moment of His existence, He knows all things.

God knows all actualities and every contingency, i.e., what has happened, what occurs now, what will happen, what would happen, what can happen, what could happen.

Since the existence of the universe, and apart from its presence, God knows and has always known everything.

Incomprehensible to the human mind is that God's highest, most profound, and most fascinating knowledge is of his being. He is infinitely deep in character, substance, beauty, and wisdom.

For the following Daily Focus meditation, focus your thoughts on the All-knowing God who knows everything about your soul, mind, and body.

Brain-talk in 100 Words

God sees and searches for me.

Why should God take the effort? Am I worth God's attention?

God finds me where I'm at and not where I think I should be—or where I think God wants me to be.

Can't run; can't hide.

I sit, giving myself away with garlic on my breath.

God sees, searches, and finds all. Right now, he pauses beside me alone in a chair.

He greets me with a smile more massive than the arc of the Milky Way creasing the sky. Catching only me in his gaze, he speaks:

"You are worth the search."

Merge Brain-talk with God-talk

Regulate your breathing and with the beads in your fingertips, speak out loud today's **Daily Focus**.

2 Chronicles 16:9 (NLT)

The eyes of the Lord search the whole earth in order to strengthen those whose hearts are fully committed to him.

God sees and searches the whole earth.

God sees and searches for me.

✝ Because of the Cross, glory to God forever.

● In the presence of God—**Father**, Son, and Holy Spirit.

● The Father sees and searches the whole earth.

⊗ Father sees and searches for me.

⊗ Father sees ⊗ and searches ⊗ for me.

● In the presence of God—Father, **Son**, and Holy Spirit.

● The Son sees and searches the whole earth.

⊗ Jesus sees and searches for me.

⊗ Jesus sees ⊗ and searches ⊗ for me.

● In the presence of God—Father, Son, and **Holy Spirit**.

● The Holy Spirit sees and searches the whole earth.

⊗ Holy Spirit sees and searches for me.

⊗ Holy Spirit sees ⊗ and searches ⊗ for me.

TWO

GOD-TALK: EVERYWHERE-PRESENT GOD

God is everywhere in the universe.

God is spirit. This means God is not bound by any physical form.

Since God is present everywhere, everything is immediately in his presence. This enables him to perfectly act everywhere (he is All-powerful) because he perfectly knows all things (he is All-knowing).

God has access to all places and all secrets all at once. No one can hide from him, and nothing escapes his notice.

For the following Daily Focus meditation, focus your thoughts on the Everywhere-present God who is here with you now for your soul, mind, and body.

Brain-talk in 100 Words

God sees my heart.

The whole earth in God's sight is a concept I barely understand. But God everywhere at the same time is something beyond cognition.

In this solitary room, I hide, tear-up, and wonder. Does God really see me? Is he really here?

If he is next to me, does he hear my diaphragm's action? Does he sense my pulse or count my heartbeats?

If God sits beside me, surely, He knows how I long for his tangible presence.

I acknowledge the tenseness of my body as I find a comfortable position. Then I relax.

He is here.

Merge Brain-talk with God-talk

Regulate your breathing and with the beads in your fingertips, speak out loud today's **Daily Focus**.

2 Chronicles 16:9 (NLT)

The eyes of the Lord search the whole earth in order to strengthen those whose hearts are fully committed to him.

God sees and finds all hearts.

God sees my heart.

✝ Because of the Cross, glory to God forever.

● In the presence of God—**Father**, Son, and Holy Spirit.

● The Father sees and finds all hearts.

⊗ Father sees my heart.

⊗ Father ⊗ sees ⊗ my heart.

● In the presence of God—Father, **Son**, and Holy Spirit.

● The Son sees and finds all hearts.

⊗ Jesus sees my heart.

⊗ Jesus ⊗ sees ⊗ my heart.

● In the presence of God—Father, Son, and **Holy Spirit**.

● The Holy Spirit sees and finds all hearts.

⊗ Holy Spirit sees my heart.

⊗ Holy Spirit ⊗ sees ⊗ my heart.

THREE

GOD-TALK: ALL-POWERFUL GOD

God has all power because God *is* the only all-powerful being in the universe. God wasn't given all power—God *is* all power.

He exercises dominion over the entire universe and beyond our universe with his power. Every bit of his power carries out the purposes as it intertwines with his character as the All-knowing, Everywhere-present and All-wise God.

All-powerful God creates all things and keeps all things in existence.

For the following Daily Focus meditation, focus your thoughts on the unlimited power of God. He creates and sustains your soul, mind, and body.

Brain-talk in 100 Words

God strengthens my heart.

It is not the organ, the fleshy pump in my chest, needing help. It's my mind and emotions and all those other immaterial elements that makeup who I am that hesitates.

A fully committed heart for God is strong, and I'm not sure mine slots into that category. I have limited objectivity when assessing my life.

Sitting still, I hear my heart beat, maybe a bit too hard and a bit too fast. But it beats with a "LUB-dub, LUB-dub" prayer for commitment:

TRUST God, TRUST God.

I permit the All-powerful God to strengthen my heart.

Merge Brain-talk with God-talk

Regulate your breathing and with the beads in your fingertips, speak out loud today's **Daily Focus**.

2 Chronicles 16:9 (NLT)

The eyes of the Lord search the whole earth in order to strengthen those whose hearts are fully committed to him.

God strengthens committed hearts.

God strengthens my heart.

✝ Because of the Cross, glory to God forever.

● In the presence of God—**Father**, Son, and Holy Spirit.

● The Father strengthens committed hearts.

⊗ Father strengthens my heart.

⊗ Father ⊗ strengthens ⊗ my heart.

● In the presence of God—Father, **Son**, and Holy Spirit.

● The Son strengthens committed hearts.

⊗ Jesus strengthens my heart.

⊗ Jesus ⊗ strengthens ⊗ my heart.

● In the presence of God—Father, Son, and **Holy Spirit**.

● The Holy Spirit strengthens committed hearts.

⊗ Holy Spirit strengthens my heart.

⊗ Holy Spirit ⊗ strengthens ⊗ my heart.

FOUR

GOD-TALK: SELF-EXISTENT GOD

The self-existence of God means that God did not and does not need us or any of his creation in order to exist. While everything else in the universe depends on God for existence, God depends on nothing but himself to exist. God's existence is of him alone.

People question their origins with "Where did I come from or who made me?" God never asks these things of himself. There is no need to.

When children ask, "Who made God?" The clearest and simplest answer is "God never needed to be made because he has always existed."

God lives in different ways from us. We exist in finite, dependent, and fragile ways. But our Maker lives in eternal, self-sustaining, and necessary ways. Necessary in this sense: God does not have it in him to go out of existence.

We do not have it in us to live forever. We necessarily age and die in our present condition. God necessarily exists as independent and unchanged because his eternal nature continues without a beginning or end.

For the following Daily Focus meditation, focus your thoughts on the self-existing God, the One who designed you to be dependent on him for your soul, mind, and body.

Brain-talk in 100 Words

God accepts my worship.

Liturgical church worship. Conservative church worship. Contemporary worship. Yes, God accepts all worship.

But I am alone, one-to-one with God, in my private space. Breathing, speaking, thinking, sparking neurons in the brain. Is this acceptable worship?

God doesn't need the crowd for his existence. Right now, I'm shy and don't do well in crowds. So, I make this moment, with my focus only on him and his focus on me, an intimate worship experience.

My praise, the thoughts that pulse with each breath, God accepts as adoration.

God accepts my worship, because...

God totally gets me.

Merge Brain-talk with God-talk

Regulate your breathing and with the beads in your fingertips, speak out loud today's **Daily Focus**.

Nehemiah 9:6

You are the LORD, you alone. You have made heaven, the heaven of heavens, with all their host, the earth and all that is on it, the seas and all that is in them; and you preserve all of them; and the host of heaven worships you.

God alone accepts worship from all creation.

God accepts my worship.

✝ Because of the Cross, glory to God forever.

● In the presence of God—**Father**, Son, and Holy Spirit.

● The Father alone accepts worship from all creation.

⊗ Father accepts my worship.

⊗ Father ⊗ accepts ⊗ my worship.

● In the presence of God—Father, **Son**, and Holy Spirit.

● The Son alone accepts worship from all creation.

⊗ Jesus accepts my worship.

⊗ Jesus ⊗ accepts ⊗ my worship.

● In the presence of God—Father, Son, and **Holy Spirit**.

● The Holy Spirit alone accepts worship from all creation.

⊗ Holy Spirit accepts my worship.

⊗ Holy Spirit ⊗ accepts ⊗ my worship.

FIVE

GOD-TALK: SELF-SUFFICIENT GOD

The Self-sufficiency of God; wording not found in Greek or Hebrew. But we understand the concept as we read the Bible.

The Self-sufficiency of God means that God does not require anything we humans need to survive: water, air, food, sleep. He does not need to bargain for anything he lacks. He lacks nothing.

God never needs counselors, supervisors, or advisors to come to his aid. God is the only being in existence who is self-sufficient in all things.

For the following Daily Focus meditation, focus your thoughts on the self-sufficiency of God, who fully and adequately ministers to your soul, mind, and body from his totally sufficient resource—himself.

Brain-talk in 100 Words

God calls for me.

When my dad yelled for me, I often knew it was for what I had done or didn't do. I remember feeling guiltier each time I heard his demand.

Authorities' calls make me sweat. I know why, too.

When the Mighty One summons me, I think as a kid, "I'm in trouble."

But God's request is a summons to be loved free from all guilt, free from any shame.

God speaks one word—my name—and I sit quietly with him. His holy and sufficient presence silences the excuses my mind brings up.

When He calls, I answer.

Merge Brain-talk with God-talk

Regulate your breathing and with the beads in your fingertips, speak out loud today's **Daily Focus**.

Psalm 50:1 (NLT)

The LORD, the Mighty One, is God, and he has spoken; he has summoned all humanity from where the sun rises to where it sets.

God calls for us; we need the Mighty One.

God calls for me.

✝ Because of the Cross, glory to God forever.

● In the presence of God—**Father**, Son, and Holy Spirit.

● The Father calls for us; we need the Mighty One.

⊗ Father calls for me.

⊗ Father ⊗ calls ⊗ for me.

● In the presence of God—Father, **Son**, and Holy Spirit.

● The Son calls for us; we need the Mighty One.

⊗ Jesus calls for me.

⊗ Jesus ⊗ calls ⊗ for me.

● In the presence of God—Father, Son, and **Holy Spirit**.

● The Holy Spirit calls for us; we need the Mighty One.

⊗ Holy Spirit calls for me.

⊗ Holy Spirit ⊗ calls ⊗ for me.

SIX

GOD-TALK: ALL-WISE GOD

God has all wisdom. He is, in his very being, all-wise. He works everything out for the good of his people for the display and enjoyment of his glory. This involves countless factors and people and events and decisions and all sorts of things that will overwhelm any mortal's mind.

Even when things look the worst in our lives, God is carrying out his perfect plan with perfect wisdom. He never fails, never lacks any foresight, and never estimates. He knows all and plans all. He loves to display the glory and beauty of his wisdom by accomplishing what we humans see as impossible.

It is not impossible for God to restore your soul. It is not impossible for God to calm your mind. It is not impossible for God to heal your body.

For the following Daily Focus meditation, focus on God's wisdom for your soul, mind, and body. He makes no mistake with your life.

Brain-talk in 100 Words

God wisely directs my paths.

I want to be a good citizen. I desire to be a good human being. But what life-path do I take to encounter life's goodness?

I don't understand enough of life to judge the best direction over misdirection.

God's wisdom declares the right way to go as he alerts me to my prejudice that prevents needless wandering. He knows I've hit dead-ends.

I look for signs, the evidence that God cares about where I go. Sometimes it's a distant flash of light; other times a close inspection at what's around me.

Wisely placed. Wisely timed.

Merge Brain-talk with God-talk

Regulate your breathing and with the beads in your fingertips, speak out loud today's **Daily Focus**.

Proverbs 5:21

For a man's ways are before the eyes of the LORD, and he ponders all his paths.

God wisely directs a person's paths.

God wisely directs my paths.

✝ Because of the Cross, glory to God forever.

● In the presence of God—**Father**, Son, and Holy Spirit.

● The Father wisely directs a person's paths.

⊗ Father wisely directs my paths.

⊗ Father ⊗ wisely directs ⊗ my path.

● In the presence of God—Father, **Son**, and Holy Spirit.

● The Son wisely directs a person's paths.

⊗ Jesus wisely directs my paths.

⊗ Jesus ⊗ wisely directs ⊗ my path.

● In the presence of God—Father, Son, and **Holy Spirit**.

● The Holy Spirit wisely directs a person's paths.

⊗ Holy Spirit wisely directs my paths.

⊗ Holy Spirit ⊗ wisely directs ⊗ my path.

SEVEN

GOD-TALK: GRACIOUS GOD

We experience God's grace when he gives us the favor that we do not deserve.

God's grace is more profound than that. It's beyond comfort and mercy. It is compatible with his justice and holiness. It is as thorough as his knowledge and as deep as his wisdom.

Grace is God acting freely, according to His nature, as love. Grace does not depend on any promises spoken by the one needing it. It is freely given because of love.

Grace is uncaused, that is, the recipient doesn't give any reason to gain grace. Its cause lies wholly in the Giver, in God.

Grace is sovereign. Once bestowed, grace is not withdrawn.

Like wisdom, the attribute of God's grace intertwines all of God's decisions about us. As with all of God's attributes, it is inexhaustible.

For the following Daily Focus meditation, focus your thoughts on the gracious God, the One who gives blessings (more than you deserve!) for your soul, mind, and body.

Brain-talk in 100 Words

God reveals his grace to me.

It may be hard to believe, but I was fooled. Especially me, I got hoodwinked.

I fell for it. I over-trusted. I was so eager to believe.

I paid the cost for foolishness. Everyone made fun of me; everyone but God.

No scolding or "You should have known better" lecture.

He saw how low I felt; so hard on myself.

It could have been worse, but he did not allow it. He pulled me from my misery.

Gracious God extends himself to gullible and simple me.

Draw in the fresh breath of God's grace.

Merge Brain-talk with God-talk

Regulate your breathing and with the beads in your fingertips, speak out loud today's **Daily Focus**.

Psalm 116:5–6

Gracious is the Lord, and righteous; our God is merciful. The Lord preserves the simple; when I was brought low, he saved me.

God reveals his essential grace to simple people.

God reveals his grace to me.

✝ Because of the Cross, glory to God forever.

● In the presence of God—**Father**, Son, and Holy Spirit.

● The Father reveals his essential grace to simple people.

⊗ Father reveals his grace to me.

⊗ Father reveals ⊗ his grace ⊗ to me.

● In the presence of God—Father, **Son**, and Holy Spirit.

● The Son reveals his essential grace to simple people.

⊗ Jesus reveals his grace to me.

⊗ Jesus reveals ⊗ his grace ⊗ to me.

● In the presence of God—Father, Son, and **Holy Spirit**.

● The Holy Spirit reveals his essential grace to simple people.

⊗ Holy Spirit reveals his grace to me.

⊗ Holy Spirit reveals ⊗ his grace ⊗ to me.

EIGHT

GOD-TALK: MERCIFUL GOD

We experience God's mercy when he withholds painful trouble from us or relieves us of suffering. Sometimes it's pain and suffering we deserve—we bring them on ourselves.

Mercy differs from grace; God administers it because it is caused by pain and suffering. God responds and relieves it with his deep-felt compassion.

People in authority express mercy when they relieve the suffering of the community under their jurisdiction. Merciful God extends mercy toward all human beings, for all of humanity is under God's authority regardless of an intimate relationship with him.

But for the one who personally knows God, the experience of God's mercy appears almost like grace. Like grace, mercy is sovereign. It is joyfully welcomed and appreciated.

To experience God's mercy is to delight in God's compassion for our traumatized minds and bodies. God knows how to relieve the pain.

For the following Daily Focus meditation, focus on God's mercy to restore your wounded soul.

Brain-talk in 100 Words

God treats me with mercy.

At six years old, I needed mercy—from Mom.

Mom had stepped out for a few minutes. It was my chance to experiment with her candy thermometer. I destroyed it. I threw away the evidence.

I then wrote a note, hung it up where Mom would see it. It said, "Stevie is a very bad boy."

When Mom found the note, I could barely talk. When she saw the evidence, she said nothing.

I wasn't hurt, although I inflicted my own pain from guilt.

God-like, Mom withheld punishment.

God extends mercy.

Resting here is proof.

Merge Brain-talk with God-talk

Regulate your breathing and with the beads in your fingertips, speak out loud today's **Daily Focus**.

Psalm 103:10

He does not deal with us according to our sins, nor repay us according to our iniquities.

God treats us with mercy when we do wrong.

God treats me with mercy.

✝ Because of the Cross, glory to God forever.

● In the presence of God—**Father**, Son, and Holy Spirit.

● The Father treats us with mercy when we do wrong.

⊗ Father treats me with mercy.

⊗ Father ⊗ treats me ⊗ with mercy.

● In the presence of God—Father, **Son**, and Holy Spirit.

● The Son treats us with mercy when we do wrong.

⊗ Jesus treats me with mercy.

⊗ Jesus ⊗ treats me ⊗ with mercy.

● In the presence of God—Father, Son, and **Holy Spirit**.

● The Holy Spirit treats us with mercy when we do wrong.

⊗ Holy Spirit treats me with mercy.

⊗ Holy Spirit ⊗ treats me ⊗ with mercy.

NINE

GOD-TALK: GOD IS JUST

We experience God's justice when he gives us what we deserve. That may not be comforting. But we do not deeply appreciate God's grace and mercy until we understand God's justice.

God's justice is his righteousness—his doing of the right things. As with all of God's attributes, justice is identical in its essence, purity, and perfection.

God is perfect grace, perfect mercy, and perfect love. As with all of God's known attributes, God cannot be less than perfect.

God's holiness causes his justice to be perfect. His holiness causes his justice to be pure. God's justice is as pure as God himself.

God wills to do only that which is right, only that which is just, and he perfectly delivers it.

God does nothing wrong to his creatures, for what he does is from the full character of his being: all-knowing, all-powerful, all-wise, everywhere-present, holy, good, and love.

God is love; he is just. God is perfect, and he is just.

For the following Daily Focus meditation, focus your thoughts on God's perfect justice perfectly delivered in pure love for your soul, mind, and body.

Brain-talk in 100 Words

God is perfectly just toward me.

Sometimes it doesn't go my way. I'll do more or pay more, and then get angry.

I might take it out on God and foolishly whine to him that I wasn't treated fairly.

"You made a mistake."

After wasting time and energy with that feeling of resentment, I cool off and recall:

I can't blame God.

God is flawless.

God is perfect.

He is perfect toward me, even when I have been treated poorly or unjustly.

God remains perfectly just as he is perfect in his love.

This focus moment is love with justice.

Merge Brain-talk with God-talk

Regulate your breathing and with the beads in your fingertips, speak out loud today's **Daily Focus**.

Deuteronomy 32:4

The Rock! His work is perfect, for all His ways are just; A God of faithfulness and without injustice, righteous and upright is He.

God is perfectly just and faithful in all his ways.

God is perfectly just toward me.

✝ Because of the Cross, glory to God forever.

● In the presence of God—**Father**, Son, and Holy Spirit.

● The Father is perfectly just and faithful in all his ways.

⊗ Father is perfectly just toward me.

⊗ Father is ⊗ perfectly just ⊗ toward me.

● In the presence of God—Father, **Son**, and Holy Spirit.

● The Son is perfectly just and faithful in all his ways.

⊗ Jesus is perfectly just toward me.

⊗ Jesus is ⊗ perfectly just ⊗ toward me.

● In the presence of God—Father, Son, and **Holy Spirit**.

● The Holy Spirit is perfectly just and faithful in all his ways.

⊗ Holy Spirit is perfectly just toward me.

⊗ Holy Spirit is ⊗ perfectly just ⊗ toward me.

TEN

GOD-TALK: UNCHANGEABLE GOD

God is immutable. That means God cannot change. God is unchangeable.

Theologian Millard Erickson called this attribute "God's constancy."

God is the only true constant being of the universe, and his unchangeableness reaches past the known universe. As small as you perceive yourself, his promises to you are as reliable as his being.

God is faithful because God is unchangeable. He is faithful to all his promises because he cannot change.

Our lives are in constant flux, but because God is unchangeable, we can be sure that

- God loves us;
- God sustains us in hard times;
- God promises unique paths for each our lives.

For the following Daily Focus meditation around the circle of beads, focus your thoughts on the absolute way God does not change his love for your soul, mind, and body.

Brain-talk in 100 Words

God fulfills his word to me.

The last time someone failed to follow through on a promise to me, I chose to be angry. Then I remembered my stumbling in a similar situation.

Others treated me better than I deserved.

I still gave out excuses. As I heard stories leave my lips, I knew they were lame.

Lame like me, crippled in the body, soul, and mind.

Depression does that. I couldn't have been more human than those moments.

This moment listen to one who is never lame and never changes.

He speaks and fulfills it.

Experience God's immutable faithfulness.

Merge Brain-talk with God-talk

Regulate your breathing and with the beads in your fingertips, speak out loud today's **Daily Focus**.

Numbers 23:19

God is not man, that he should lie, or a son of man, that he should change his mind. Has he said, and will he not do it? Or has he spoken, and will he not fulfill it?

God unchangeable fulfills his word to us.

God fulfills his word to me.

✝ Because of the Cross, glory to God forever.

● In the presence of God—**Father**, Son, and Holy Spirit.

● The Father unchangeable fulfills his word to us.

⊗ Father fulfills his word to me.

⊗ Father fulfills ⊗ his word ⊗ to me.

● In the presence of God—Father, **Son**, and Holy Spirit.

● The Son unchangeable fulfills his word to us.

⊗ Jesus fulfills his word to me.

⊗ Jesus fulfills ⊗ his word ⊗ to me.

● In the presence of God—Father, Son, and **Holy Spirit**.

● The Holy Spirit unchangeable fulfills his word to us.

⊗ Holy Spirit fulfills his word to me.

⊗ Holy Spirit fulfills ⊗ his word ⊗ to me.

ELEVEN

GOD-TALK: ETERNAL GOD

The adjective aionios in New Testament Greek translates as "eternal." Eternal means there is no obvious beginning or end. Classic Greek philosophers of the Mediterranean defined eternity as what exists outside of time. When the New Testament writers described God as eternal, they revealed God as endless in duration, having no beginning and no end outside of time.

The Bible also describes something else eternal: human souls.

We human beings are made in the image of God. We have an awareness of eternity within our souls because God made us that way. We cannot fully comprehend our eternal character, but we sense it. It remains mysterious to us.

We can't measure our eternal nature like our blood pressures and temperatures. When we try to describe it with words anchored in the temporal, as if it can be touched, we confuse ourselves. We say things like, "forever (eternity) is a long time" when eternity means that there is no time at all.

Almost a thousand years ago, Anselm of Canterbury said of God, "He exists before all things and transcends all things, even the eternal things."

God is greater than his creation in the physical and non-physical universe. He reigns over time and timelessness. He created us for both his glory and our enjoyment with God—within time and outside of time.

For the following Daily Focus meditation around the circle of beads, focus your thoughts on eternal God who shares his very nature with your soul, mind, and body.

Brain-talk in 100 Words

God's eternal life is my life.

God shares his eternal being to enhance human life. Eternality improves life because it is God's life.

Physical or temporal constraints cannot bind eternal God. He is without beginning, without end, and without measure. That is eternal life.

We lack enough English words describing the eternal. Eternal life is God sharing his immeasurable life.

I issued one deliberate thought in exchange for the unfathomable enhancement of God's boundless life.

I gained more than peace from God in that transaction; I gained God's eternal life!

Now that is a concept worth lots of brain time.

Merge Brain-talk with God-talk

Regulate your breathing and with the beads in your fingertips, speak out loud today's **Daily Focus**.

John 3:15–16 (NASB)

Whoever believes will in Him have eternal life. For God so loved the world, that He gave His only begotten Son, that whoever believes in Him shall not perish, but have eternal life.

God's eternal being is life for believers.

God's eternal life is my life.

✝ Because of the Cross, glory to God forever.

● In the presence of God—**Father**, Son, and Holy Spirit.

● The Father's eternal being is life for believers.

⊗ Father's eternal life is my life.

⊗ Father's ⊗ eternal life ⊗ is my life.

● In the presence of God—Father, **Son**, and Holy Spirit.

● The Son's eternal being is life for believers.

⊗ Jesus' eternal life is my life.

⊗ Jesus' life ⊗ eternal life ⊗ is my life.

● In the presence of God—Father, Son, and **Holy Spirit**.

● The Holy Spirit's eternal being is life for believers.

⊗ Holy Spirit's eternal life is my life.

⊗ Holy Spirit's ⊗ eternal life ⊗ is my life.

TWELVE

GOD-TALK: INFINITE GOD

God's attribute of eternity is similar to God's quality of infinity. Likewise, it is beyond our human ability to grasp it fully.

Like eternity, infinity has no measurable beginning or end. Unlike eternity, it is within time and space. Infinity is immeasurable in quantity, amount, and number.

In a limited form, we display God's limitlessness. In a finite way, as *imago Dei* (image of God), our design reflects God's infinite nature.

Mathematicians scribe chalkboards full of equations and symbols with proofs for infinity. Artists design fractal images that endlessly replicate original patterns. But the best example of human infinity is from the perspective of the collective human race.

Our DNA sequencing makes it possible for physical and epigenetic traits to pop up with infinite combinations when males and females mate and reproduce. With all the billions of people on the earth (past, present, and future) the human population exploded according to God's design of infinity. From one set of created parents, whom God commanded to "multiply and fill the earth," God's infinite nature gets a showing. But because of sin, individual humans cannot forever live and reproduce. They die.

Death of the human creation is the separation of the soul from the body. But God cannot die. God is and has always been, immortal. His infinite nature is perfect, so in contrast to human lives, we cannot display absolute infinity.

The Bible repeatedly makes this life/death contrast between the children of Adam and God. God reveals his infinity to us by his immortality. But God promises that there will be a time when our mortal bodies must put on immortality.

For the next circles around the beads, focus your thoughts on the infinite and immortal God who shares his infinite nature with your soul, mind, and body.

Brain-talk in 100 Words

God immortal rules over my life.

My life is like a camera's flash compared to God's visible and invisible light beams. Though I flash on then off, my life expresses God's plan to reflect his infinite nature.

I possess unlimited possibilities to honor and praise God by living for God. Even my slightest breaths and smallest thoughts can give God glory.

I rest my life in God's hands, and he is satisfied to be my King, the immortal Lord of the universe.

Honor and praise the King!

I live for the King to express boundless praise with a mortal body.

Merge Brain-talk with God-talk

Regulate your breathing and with the beads in your fingertips, speak out loud today's **Daily Focus**.

1 Timothy 1:17

To the King of the ages, immortal, invisible, the only God, be honor and glory forever and ever. Amen.

God immortal rules over transient life.

God immortal rules over my life.

✝ Because of the Cross, glory to God forever.

● In the presence of God—**Father**, Son, and Holy Spirit.

● The Father immortal rules over transient life.

⊗ Father immortal rules over my life.

⊗ Father immortal ⊗ rules over ⊗ my life.

● In the presence of God—Father, **Son**, and Holy Spirit.

● The Son immortal rules over transient life.

⊗ Jesus immortal rules over my life.

⊗ Jesus immortal ⊗ rules over ⊗ my life.

● In the presence of God—Father, Son, and **Holy Spirit**.

● The Holy Spirit immortal rules over transient life.

⊗ Holy Spirit immortal rules over my life.

⊗ Holy Spirit immortal ⊗ rules over ⊗ my life.

THIRTEEN

GOD-TALK: GOD IS LOVE

God does not merely love or act lovingly. God's very being is love.

Humans can act lovingly, but humans cannot say they personify love as the essence of their being. Only God can say that his very existence is love. God is love and continues to love even when his creation rejects him.

The love of God is best to be experienced rather than reasoned. The mystery of why God loves humanity is not solved, but it can be explored. Humans are *imago Dei* (image of God), and God loves his creation. But there is a bigger mystery.

God loves God. This is not narcissism. This is how God holds the universe together. It is the mystery of the Trinity—Father, Son, and Holy Spirit.

God's love for the world is inexhaustible. God cannot be exhausted of his love, for God cannot exhaust himself of his being.

For the following Daily Focus meditation, focus your thoughts on how God is love and loves you—your soul, mind, and body.

Brain-talk in 100 Words

God loves me.

Three simple words sum up the significant pull of this truth. These words are as plain as it gets.

Did you expect difficult? Add three more words.

God is love.

When describing deep relationships between couples in love, people say things like "It's complicated."

Our love relationship with God is not complicated. Even if we don't return love, God keeps it simple.

These words are carved in stone, etched on legal parchment, and impressed on your heart. Sense them in your soul to discover the simplicity.

Combine them. Experience them.

God is love.

God loves me.

Deeply ... breathe ... those ... words.

Merge Brain-talk with God-talk

Regulate your breathing and with the beads in your fingertips, speak out loud today's **Daily Focus**.

1 John 4:7–8

Beloved let us love one another, for love is from God ... because God is love.

God loves us because God is love.

God loves me.

✝ Because of the Cross, glory to God forever.

● In the presence of God—**Father**, Son, and Holy Spirit.

● The Father loves us because God is love.

⊗ Father loves me.

⊗ Father ⊗ loves ⊗ me.

● In the presence of God—Father, **Son**, and Holy Spirit.

● The Son loves us because God is love.

⊗ Jesus loves me.

⊗ Jesus ⊗ loves ⊗ me.

● In the presence of God—Father, Son, and **Holy Spirit**.

● The Holy Spirit loves us because God is love.

⊗ Holy Spirit loves me.

⊗ Holy Spirit ⊗ loves ⊗ me.

FOURTEEN

GOD-TALK: GOD IS GOOD

In C.S. Lewis' *The Lion, the Witch, and the Wardrobe* from his *Chronicles of Narnia* fantasy series, Susan and Lucy learn from the Beavers about Aslan, the powerful lion representing Christ. If they were to meet him, they ask if Aslan is safe.

"Safe?" said Mr. Beaver. "Who said anything about safe? 'Course he isn't safe. But he's good."

God is good. Like all of God's attributes, God's goodness is perfect in essence, consistency, and purity. God is always good to us even when we experience discomfort from evil attacks and tragic events.

The goodness of God is the personality of God behind his other attributes. He is good in his intentions, motives, and actions as the all-powerful, just, holy, and merciful God. Even when non-perceptible, God's actions are always and at all times good. It is impossible for God to act in any bad or evil way.

God's goodness is absolute. Like all of his characteristics, God's goodness is pure and righteous. As his love and holiness are perfect, his goodness is perfect.

"There is only one who is good," said Jesus referring to God the Father and himself.

For the following Daily Focus meditation around the circle of beads, focus your thoughts on the absolute reality that God is good for your soul, mind, and body.

Brain-talk in 100 Words

God is good to me.

Eternality is the unfathomable concept of no-time.

When I talk about life as eternal, I don't mean biological life. I speak of *zōē*, God's imparted life that blends human souls with him.

Here's why God provides eternal life: God is good.

God is good not in the sense of sugary sweetness and niceness. God is good because his intentions are only for good.

God doesn't push; he leads.

He invites a following. It's an exclusively good invitation.

Spark new thoughts with each bead because eternal life is supremely good.

God's life becomes our superb life.

Merge Brain-talk with God-talk

Regulate your breathing and with the beads in your fingertips, speak out loud today's **Daily Focus**.

Matthew 19:16–21 (NKJV)

Now behold, one came and said to Him, "Good Teacher, what good thing shall I do that I may have eternal life?" So He said to him, "Why do you call Me good? No one is good but One, that is, God. But if you want to enter into life, keep the commandments ... and come, follow Me."

God is good and provides us eternal life.

God is good to me.

✝ Because of the Cross, glory to God forever.

● In the presence of God—**Father**, Son, and Holy Spirit.

● The Father is good and provides us eternal life.

⊗ Father is good to me.

⊗ Father ⊗ is good ⊗ to me.

● In the presence of God—Father, **Son**, and Holy Spirit.

● The Son is good and provides us eternal life.

⊗ Jesus is good to me.

⊗ Jesus ⊗ is good ⊗ to me.

● In the presence of God—Father, Son, and **Holy Spirit**.

● The Holy Spirit is good and provides us eternal life.

⊗ Holy Spirit is good to me.

⊗ Holy Spirit ⊗ is good ⊗ to me.

FIFTEEN

GOD-TALK: GOD IS HOLY

God declares that he is holy. The people of God proclaim God as holy. God commands the people of God to be holy as he is holy.

To be holy is to be separate and set apart. God is separate from all that is not God. God commands the people of God to be separate from all that pollutes life and diminishes their integrity as the image of God.

In the Old Testament, God set apart Israel as a people for his own purpose. In the New Testament, God sets apart people and indwells them by the Holy Spirit.

All of God's acts and all of his actions express his absolute character of being: holy. There is also nothing in the universe that can diminish God's holiness since he is separate from his creation. God is holy for God is pure and pristine.

For the next circles around the beads, focus your thoughts on the holiness of God and how he shares his pure and holy nature with your soul, mind, and body.

Brain-talk in 100 Words

God, Holy King, created me.

My life started when chromosomes of XY and XX paired up making me unique. No one else in creation possesses my DNA blend.

My unshared separateness from all others who bear the image of God tells the universe that I belong to the Creator, King of the Universe. From a distance or under a microscope, I am set apart and under his jurisdiction.

I was created to be set apart—holy—though I am not yet pure as the Creator is pure.

The King is working on that.

Breathe deep to honor the Holy King.

Merge Brain-talk with God-talk

Regulate your breathing and with the beads in your fingertips, speak out loud today's **Daily Focus**.

Isaiah 43:15

"I am the Lord, your Holy One, the Creator of Israel, your King.

God, our Holy King, created unique people.

God, Holy King, created me.

✝ Because of the Cross, glory to God forever.

● In the presence of God—**Father**, Son, and Holy Spirit.

● The Father, our Holy King, created unique people.

⊗ Father, Holy King, created me.

⊗ Father ⊗ Holy King ⊗ created me.

● In the presence of God—Father, **Son**, and Holy Spirit.

● The Son, our Holy King, created unique people.

⊗ Jesus, Holy King, created me.

⊗ Jesus ⊗ Holy King ⊗ created me.

● In the presence of God—Father, Son, and **Holy Spirit**.

● The Holy Spirit, our Holy King, created unique people.

⊗ Holy Spirit, Holy King, created me.

⊗ Holy Spirit ⊗ Holy King ⊗ created me.

SIXTEEN

GOD-TALK: TRUTHFUL GOD

Referred to as the veracity of God is the attribute of the truthfulness of God. God has a pure and absolute devotion to the truth and the power to convey the truth. The truthfulness of God is simple:

God tells the truth because God IS truth.

God's truthfulness means that God cannot be untruthful. God cannot lie; it is against his nature to lie.

God did not lie when He etched in original stone autographs (The Ten Commandments) or when he used various writers to author histories, narratives, poetries, prophecies, and promises. Errors allegedly found in the Bible are those of the scribes making copies of what God previously communicated. Therefore, the truthfulness of God is never impugned.

What God communicates is never false. What God says equals to what God is.

For the next Daily Focus meditation, focus on how God communicates his truthfulness concerning your soul, mind, and body.

Brain-talk in 100 Words

God tells me the truth.

God speaks only the truth. He speaks the absolute truth.

Absolute truth is that which is true for all people at all times in all places.

To hold opinions about God without accepting the premise of absolute truth is to be prejudiced against God. That's a frustrating way think. That was my youthful downfall.

I denied absolute truth and welcomed all kinds of lies to me and about me.

What God says about me is the truth about me.

What God says about God is the truth about God.

Breathe to speak the absolute truth.

Merge Brain-talk with God-talk

Regulate your breathing and with the beads in your fingertips, speak out loud today's **Daily Focus**.

John 14:6

Jesus said to him, "I am the way, and the truth, and the life. No one comes to the Father except through me."

God declares that he is absolute truth.

God tells me the truth.

✝ Because of the Cross, glory to God forever.

● In the presence of God—**Father**, Son, and Holy Spirit.

● The Father declares that he is absolute truth.

⊗ Father tells me the truth.

⊗ Father ⊗ tells me ⊗ the truth.

● In the presence of God—Father, **Son**, and Holy Spirit.

● The Son declares that he is absolute truth.

⊗ Jesus tells me the truth.

⊗ Jesus ⊗ tells me ⊗ the truth.

● In the presence of God—Father, Son, and **Holy Spirit**.

● The Holy Spirit declares that he is absolute truth.

⊗ Holy Spirit tells me the truth.

⊗ Holy Spirit ⊗ tells me ⊗ the truth.

SEVENTEEN

GOD-TALK: TRANSCENDENT GOD

God is wholly independent of the material universe. He is beyond all physical laws ranging from the microcosm of sub-atomic particles to the macrocosm of the galaxies making up our universe. He is beyond what can be conceived as the multi-universe, and all that is beyond our limited understanding of existence.

Almost a thousand years ago, Anselm of Canterbury composed a significant work on the proof of God's existence. In this masterpiece, he wrote, "God is that than which a greater cannot be conceived."

God's attribute of transcendence tells us that God is beyond our thinking and greater than we can think. God bridges all the gaps and gulfs which span material distances and intangible components. No matter our physical, mental, or spiritual condition in life, he reaches out to us with but one motive: his loves for us.

God is beyond all time and space, so for the following Daily Focus meditation, focus on how he reaches to your soul, mind, and body.

Brain-talk in 100 Words

God looks to dwell with me.

I interpreted God's silence as God ignoring me.

With no audible voice, he spoke. His muteness revealed my true plight.

"I'm not ignoring you. I'm living in you," said the silence.

I complained of pain. He hushed me with an answer. His compassion cried within me.

My whining about financial hardship—again—exhibited my forgetfulness about God's compensation to me. He's not living rent-free. It cost him much to reside in my being.

God enjoys plain dwellings which lack deluxe amenities, especially when they're broken.

In his silence, God attends to his humbled property.

Merge Brain-talk with God-talk

Regulate your breathing and with the beads in your fingertips, speak out loud today's **Daily Focus**.

Isaiah 66:1–2

Thus says the Lord: "Heaven is my throne, and the earth is my footstool ... what is the place of my rest? ... But this is the one to whom I will look: he who is humble and contrite in spirit and trembles at my word.

God looks to dwell with humbled people.

God looks to dwell with me.

✝ Because of the Cross, glory to God forever.

● In the presence of God—**Father**, Son, and Holy Spirit.

● The Father looks to dwell with humbled people.

⊗ Father looks to dwell with me.

⊗ Father looks ⊗ to dwell ⊗ with me.

● In the presence of God—Father, **Son**, and Holy Spirit.

● The Son looks to dwell with humbled people.

⊗ Jesus looks to dwell with me.

⊗ Jesus looks ⊗ to dwell ⊗ with me.

● In the presence of God—Father, Son, and **Holy Spirit**.

● The Holy Spirit looks to dwell with humbled people.

⊗ Holy Spirit looks to dwell with me.

⊗ Holy Spirit looks ⊗ to dwell ⊗ with me.

EIGHTEEN

GOD-TALK: SOVEREIGN GOD

All things exist under God's rule and control. Nothing exists or operates without his direction or permission.

God is God. God is sovereign to declare that God is God.

He is sovereign in all his activities, over all authorities, and through all events in time and space. He is sovereign apart from time and space.

In all of God's attributes covered in this book, his sovereignty shines as the premise—the foundation of his being. He is sovereign in his All-knowing, All-powerful, and Everywhere-present self. He evidences his sovereignty by his immutability, his holiness, and his love. God's character is pure grace, mercy, and justice which he displays to us in interactive sovereignty.

We don't make him sovereign in our lives; he IS sovereign.

For the following Daily Focus meditation, focus on how God is sovereign over your soul, mind, and body.

Brain-talk in 100 Words

God reigns supreme over me.

Did your job end abruptly? Did tragedy take loved ones?

It's hard to say "God is in control" when cruel events whisk away joy.

I admit to mumbling a doubtful praise, "God is in control."

Dark thoughts slipped into my mind like cold drafts into a slightly heated room and coaxed out more doubts.

"He has forgotten me."

"He's too busy for me."

"He doesn't seem to care."

But declare it by faith: "God reigns supreme."

Breathe a testimony and defy the darkness that cannot dim eternal light.

The Sovereign Lord rules the universe—forever.

Merge Brain-talk with God-talk

Regulate your breathing and with the beads in your fingertips, speak out loud today's **Daily Focus**.

Revelation 11:15

The kingdom of the world has become the kingdom of our Lord and of his Christ, and he shall reign forever and ever.

God reigns supreme over the world forever.

God reigns supreme over me.

✝ Because of the Cross, glory to God forever.

● In the presence of God—**Father**, Son, and Holy Spirit.

● The Father reigns supreme over the world forever.

⊗ Father reigns supreme over me.

⊗ Father ⊗ reigns supreme ⊗ over me.

● In the presence of God—Father, **Son**, and Holy Spirit.

● The Son reigns supreme over the world forever.

⊗ Jesus reigns supreme over me.

⊗ Jesus ⊗ reigns supreme ⊗ over me.

● In the presence of God—Father, Son, and **Holy Spirit**.

● The Holy Spirit reigns supreme over the world forever.

⊗ Holy Spirit reigns supreme over me.

⊗ Holy Spirit ⊗ reigns supreme ⊗ over me.

After 18 Consecutive Days

If you meditated 18 consecutive days with a new Daily Focus each day, then repeat the routine for the next 18 days beginning with the first one. Return to Daily Focus ONE and repeat the process through from All-knowing God to Sovereign God. Continue to the end for another 18 days. Make notes of how you think differently about God with the second journey through God's attributes.

After 36 Days Consecutive

Whether you meditated with option one or two, it is my hope and prayer that you have seen improvement in your mental health.

Do you sleep better? Are your thoughts about God much more improved?

As you continue to meditate with the Daily Focus meditations, how have your thoughts changed? How has your brain changed?

Many more Daily Focus meditations are waiting for you. Visit me at RestoringYourSoul.com.

FINAL THOUGHTS

WHY YOU HESITATE

North American churches have perceived Christian mysticism and Eastern religions with earned suspicion. More harm than good comes to people who give up on the Christian faith in order to find a method that promises the serenity they need. For people in depression, no amount of Bible study and prayer bring relief, so as injured souls, they look outside the community of faith to find a tranquil lifestyle. But it's a dangerous trade-off.

I list the most popular meditation practices marketed to North American cultures with this warning: They are without Scriptural foundations and void of the theological truths of God's attributes and God as the Trinity.

With the wisdom God imparts to you by the Holy Spirit, discern truth from error. Compare them to the methods and truths taught in *Brain-talk Meets God-talk*.

Eastern Religions' Mysticism and Meditation

Since the 1960s, the gurus and maharishis not only claimed meditation as a way to peace with the universe, they also filled their bank accounts with the monies from desperate people who wanted personal peace. Here is a basic list of what they currently offer at a price beyond spendable cash.

Focused Attention Meditation. This promotes attention to a single object or action: a breath, a mantra, visualization, a part of the body, or a candle. It is sometimes promoted as a detachment from the world and one's desires to be free from the stress of the world.

Open Monitoring Meditation. This is passive observance without judgments of all attitudes and perspectives during the meditation experience. It incorporates all the senses without moral reasoning. Ironically, its purpose is to get you to lose touch with your sense of self, emotions, and thoughts while submerged in "awareness."

These meditation practices do not come from either the Old Testament or New Testament of the Bible. They come from religions that claim to be more ancient than Judaism, but they are not. They claim to have invented meditation, but they did not. They are imitators and offer false spirituality. These methods may relieve stress, but they don't resolve neurological disorders or offer timeless truths.

Roots in Hinduism

Mantra meditation

- Yoga
    - Kundalini meditation is the awakening of psychic energies in the body. It is the discovery of one's Third Eye and the release of sacred energy in the body—the Chakra. This is a perilous practice. There is no guard against invisible and evil forces ready to use willing hosts who suspend thinking and judgment to experience rushes of energy.
    - Gazing and Sound (Nada Yoga)
- Transcendental Meditation (TM)

  Mantras spoken in meditation are supposed to be "meaningless words" to one's ears and mind. These vocal utterances are to inhibit brain activity and give rest to the stressed-out brain. But the "meaningless words" are often names that belong to any of the three million Hindu gods. To empty the mind and transcend above is the appeal of TM.

Roots in Buddhism

- The "Om" sound for meditation.

  The "Om" meets the requirement for the utterance of a one-syllable word that is repeated to help meditation. This is observed in Buddhism, Jainism, Sikhism, and Taoism.

- Zen (Zazen) meditation.
- This technique focuses one's attention on the breath and all aspects of breathing. As Zen is to free people from their desires, meditation is the means to stifle and detach from desires, especially the desires that create unwanted stress.
- Vipassana ("Clear insight") meditation.
  This requires focused attention to one's breathing and surroundings. It is the foundation of the popularized Mindfulness meditation.
- Mindfulness meditation.
  The Buddhist term *sati* means "awareness." *Anapanasati* is "mindfulness of breathing." This is the awareness of being "in the moment" and how the senses relate to the immediate surroundings. From Mindfulness.org, "Mindfulness is the basic human ability to be fully present, aware of where we are and what we're doing, and not overly reactive or overwhelmed by what's going on around us." It sounds attractive, but Mindfulness teachers emphasize the liberty to let the mind wander and discover new things to contemplate and admire about yourself without a focus on God.

Chinese Taoism

- Taoism (influenced by Buddhism)
  Like its relative in Zen, a practitioner empties the mind of desires. It advocates for visualization of one's place in the universe. This meditation is often utilized in Chinese martial arts.
- Qigong (Chi kung)
  This is the "life energy cultivation" of one's inner energy. It was not at first a religious practice, but I include it in this list because Buddhism has hijacked it. On its own and before the introduction of Buddhism, it was a way of healing and health in Chinese science. Just as chemistry

in medications is promoted in western countries, Qigong was to cultivate and balance the body's inner energy for health and wellbeing. But the meditative practice became Buddhist Qigong to encourage a path to spiritual enlightenment.

Christian Mysticism and Contemplation

Calling it Contemplative Prayer and Detachment, Christian mystics like Meister Eckhart (1260–1328) and Pierre Teilhard de Chardin (1881–1955) influenced even the New Age movement. But their methods had the effect of isolating wounded souls rather than healing them to bring them back into the fellowship of believers. Their methods fit well for people who had already disengaged from life because of depression.

RESTORING YOUR SOUL

No matter how teachers of other meditation practices phrase it, at the center of all these types of foreign contemplation is one's self. Mindfulness, which is sometimes promoted by Christian mental health counseling services, focusses on what you are aware of and doing in the moment.

Though the meditation method laid out in *Brain-talk Meets God-talk* includes you, you are not the focus in meditation. God is your focus. Furthermore, good thoughts about our Triune God sharpen your focus. In turn, God reveals how he has always focused on you but now wants to draw you closer and tighter in his loving grip. This creates not only good neurological activity for the brain (neuroplasticity and the suppressed activity of the amygdala) it also promotes wholesome and holy worship for your private devotional time.

Many types of meditation can lead you astray from the faith. You end up serving yourself with a type of worship by looking only at yourself—a substitute for worshiping God. The LORD (Yahweh) calls that idolatry.

The Apostle John ended his first letter to first-century Christians with this exhortation, "Little children, keep yourself from idols." This has been foremost in my mind and heart as I developed this new method of meditation.

May God's love for you be compounded as you learn to meditate on him who is perfect LOVE. May you increase in your love for God as you faithfully enjoy the meditative practice promoted in *Brain-talk Meets God-talk*. My intention is for you to allow God to restore your peace and restore your soul, mind, and body.

Let this be your declaration, in the present tense, as it was for David the Psalmist:

"He restores my soul."

HELPFUL BOOKS

Brain-talk Meets God-talk is not a scholarly or research manual, but the experts in neurology and theology offer excellent bibliographies included in their books.

Bibliography

Burt, Gabor George. *Slingshot: Re-imagine your business, re-imagine your life*, Franklin Green Publishing, 2011.

Eliot, T.S. *The Wasteland*, 1922, public domain 1998.

Jennings, Timothy *The God-shaped Brain: How changing your view of God transforms your life*, Intervarsity Press, 2013.

Leaf, Caroline. *Switch On Your Brain: The Key to Peak Happiness, Thinking, and Health*, Baker Books, 2013.

Merton, Thomas. *Thoughts In Solitude, Prayer of Abandonment.* New York: Farrar, Straus and Giroux, 1958.

Newberg, Andrew. *How God Changes Your Brain: Breakthrough Findings from a Leading Neuroscientist*, Ballantine Books, 2009.

Simpson, Amy. *Troubled Minds: Mental Illness and the Church's Mission*, Intervarsity Press, 2013.

Steinbeck, John. *Travels With Charley: In Search of America*, New York: Viking Press, 1962

Extra Reading

Anselm of Durham. *Proslogion,* www.LogosLibrary.org/anselm/proslogion

Augustine of Hippo. *On the Holy Trinity,* www.NewAdvent.org/fathers/

INTERNET SHOUT OUTS

www.AmySimpson.com
www.AndrewNewberg.com
www.BrettUllman.com
www.ComeAndReason.com (Dr. Timothy Jennings)
www.Coptic.net. (Anthony the Great of Egypt)
www.GaborGeorgeBurt.com
www.gty.org/library/articles/A215/our-triune-god
www.LifeLoveAndFamily.org/ (Dr. Tim Clinton)
www.nndc.org (National Network of Depression Centers)
www.theopedia.com/attributes-of-god
www.TimClinton.com

INDEX OF SCRIPTURE VERSES

In the order of usage for the Daily Focus meditations:

ABOUT THE AUTHOR

Steve Baker has a life-long service for Jesus Christ in the United States, Canada, Africa, Mexico, and, most recently, Russia. After graduating with a B.A. from the University of Iowa, he joined a mission agency where he met his wife, Kathy. Steve assisted in Bible translation projects, teaching literacy, technical writing, and anything else English majors might do in obedience to the Great Commission.

Steve and Kathy have 3 adult children all born outside the United States. They are well balanced TCKs (Third Culture Kids).

Missionary service has its share of trauma. It is an occupational hazard. Rough living in the jungle of Liberia, West Africa, included tropical sicknesses and political turmoil—normal life in the 1980s. Life changed after the Baker family evacuated from Liberia when the country's bloody civil war started. After a decade in Chihuahua, Mexico, Steve and Kathy settled in Des Moines, Iowa.

In the summer of 2006, Steve endured a horrific bicycle vs truck crash. (Steve was the bicyclist.) He endured years of pain with additional mental and emotional traumas. During his career as a content-management technical writer, in 2015 he began a stretch of two years with major, clinical depression. During his darkest times, with perpetual anxiety attacks, he kept studying God's Word, church history, and selected books on neurology. As a result, he wrote the Daily Focus meditations and developed the meditation method that pulled him out of darkness.

WHAT'S NEXT?

Brain-talk Meets God-talk is your introductory book that contains instructions and enough Daily Focus meditations to get you started on a life-changing journey. If you meditate for 30 or more consecutive days, you will know if your investment in this book and beads was wise.

You can add to your investment with more Daily Focus meditations to help you grow deeper in your discipline to meditate.

For resources, such as Anglican prayer beads, vlogs, blogs, and videos, connect at **RestoringYourSoul.com.**

Get the eBook and the Audiobook!